The Silmarillion
–
Thirty Years On

edited by Allan Turner

2007

Cormarë Series

No 15

Series Editors
Peter Buchs • Thomas Honegger • Andrew Moglestue

Editor responsible for this volume:
Peter Buchs

Library of Congress Cataloging-in-Publication Data

Turner, Allan (editor)

The Silmarillion – Thirty Years On

ISBN 978-3-905703-10-8

Subject headings:

Tolkien, J. R. R. (John Ronald Reuel), 1892-1973 – Criticism and interpretation
Tolkien, J. R. R. (John Ronald Reuel), 1892-1973 – Language
Fantasy fiction, English – History and criticism
Middle-earth (Imaginary place)
Literature, Comparative.

Cover artwork by Anke Eissmann.

All rights reserved. No portion of this book may be reproduced, by any process or technique, without the express written consent of the publisher.

Table of Contents

Allan Turner
Preface

Rhona Beare
A Mythology for England   1

Michael Drout
Reflections on Thirty Years of Reading *The Silmarillion*   33

Anna Slack
Moving Mandos:
The Dynamics of Subcreation in 'Of Beren and Lúthien'   59

Michaël Devaux
The Origins of the *Ainulindalë*:
The Present State of Research   81

Jason Fisher
From Mythopoeia to Mythography:
Tolkien, Lönnrot, and Jerome   111

Nils Ivar Agøy
Viewpoints, Audiences and Lost Texts in *The Silmarillion*   139

Preface

If *The Lord of the Rings* came "like lightning from a clear sky", the publication of *The Silmarillion* in 1977 was a long-awaited event for readers of Tolkien. It had been common knowledge among insiders that he was working on a book of this name. The Preface to *The Adventures of Tom Bombadil* and the linguistic notes accompanying the song cycle *The Road Goes Ever On* had been tantalising snippets suggesting that there was much more to be known about the pre-history and mythology that could be glimpsed in the larger work. When Tolkien died in 1973 with the "new" book still unpublished, many thought that now Morgoth and Túrin would remain mere names. When it was announced that the book was being prepared for publication by Christopher Tolkien, the relief was great.

However, the initial excitement when it finally appeared was followed in many cases by disappointment or incomprehension. The tales contained little conversation and certainly no hobbit-like humour; indeed, they were unremittingly grim and tragic. The narrative viewpoint was remote and the recounting of events so condensed that it was hard for readers to feel a sense of involvement. Eric Korn, reviewing the book in the Times Literary Supplement,[1] was in no doubt. Referring to Christopher Tolkien's statement that there was still a wealth of material to be published, he commented: "That was the good news: the bad news is that it is unreadable."

The reception of *The Silmarillion* has been complicated since then by the appearance first of *Unfinished Tales* and then of the monumental *History of Middle-earth*, which have made it clear that the legends of the First Age were much more fluid and varied than the original lapidary version suggests. Even if they do not display the variation and metamorphosis that might be expected in a primary world mythology, nevertheless the range of texts, from the epic poetry of the *Lay of the Children of Húrin* to the Platonic

---

[1] 30th September 1977, p. 1097.

dialogue of the *Athrabeth*, conveys a cultural world not much less vital, even if narrower and more remote, than that of *The Lord of the Rings*. In turn, however, by virtue of its status as the first and most unified form of the mythology, the 1977 *Silmarillion* stands out in the midst of this fascinating but rather unstable corpus as the canonical work, the standard against which all variations are measured.

The present selection of articles is intended as a celebration of the publication thirty years ago of what can be seen in retrospect as a cardinal point in our understanding of what lay at the heart of Tolkien's imagination, the mythical kernel without which the story of the One Ring would have been deprived of a large part of its depth. Although they may show in passing the ways in which the 'Silmarillions' contribute to our critical understanding, nevertheless they all take as their fixed point the 1977 *Silmarillion*, either to demonstrate how it came into being as a text or else to show how it embodies as a work of literature Tolkien's unique blend of scholarship and the inner life of the spirit.

Walking Tree's original plan was to celebrate the occasion by re-publishing Rhona Beare's booklet on *The Silmarillion*, which had gone out of print. This originally appeared in a series for readers of science fiction and was designed to serve as an introduction to the world of the mythology, assuming no previous knowledge of Tolkien's scholarly and creative world. It is remarkable for its lucidity of expression, explaining the complexities of Tolkien's vision in language that is simple throughout but never simplistic. The book's insights benefit from Rhona Beare's long familiarity with the material. It will be remembered that she corresponded with Tolkien about points in the background to *The Lord of the Rings* which she felt required some clarification; indeed, Tolkien wrote for her (although he did not send it) a significant draft of the story of Aulë's creation of the dwarves and their receiving independent life through the grace of Eru (no. 211 in the published *Letters*). However, readers of WTP publications would not normally need an introduction to Tolkien's writing, and anyway there can be few people who know nothing at all about Middle-earth since the success of Peter Jackson's films. Therefore it was decided to take a section of the book and make it the nucleus of the collection of articles that is presented here. In the event, Rhona Beare has undertaken a thorough revision of the part of her book which elaborates the spirit of Northernness (Anglo-Saxon in the main, though touching on Celtic) running through the mythology. A significant new piece of research is her exploration of the word *earendel* and its meaning as demonstrated in the *Blickling Homilies*.

Michael Drout's contribution also takes up once again the theme of Tolkien's philological scholarship as an influence on his thought, this time to restore legitimacy to a concept that has fallen into disrepute with many critics: nostalgia. In doing this, he sets the study against the background of his childhood experience of reading and reacting to *The Silmarillion*. Academics are as a rule notoriously unwilling to acknowledge the inner sources of their insights, preferring to hide behind a smoke-screen of scientific objectivity. Here Michael Drout has the courage to expose the pain and solace of the child in order to relate it with scholarly rigour to the representation of emotions in the face of adversity as found on the one hand in the Old English *Beowulf* and *The Wanderer*, and on the other in the Men and Elves who held out against the power of Morgoth in a resistance which is shown to be vain from the outset. For him, this is a history in which, unlike in *The Lord of the Rings*, the consolation of eucatastrophe is rare, unconvincing, and perhaps not even appropriate.

Anna Slack, in contrast, finds numerous examples of eucatastrophe in 'Of Beren and Lúthien', which is undoubtedly the tale with the greatest resemblance to the traditional fairy-story, possibly because of this very quality. She shows how these sudden turns in fortune are often precipitated by performative acts, in particular song, which she sees as an indirect link to the Music of the Ainur, the primal sub-creative act in the eternal, timeless region outside the circles of the world which underlies the whole 'Heilsgeschichte' of Arda.

The last three articles are concerned with the construction of a text. To continue with the idea of the Music of the Ainur, Michaël Devaux presents an overview of research on the *Ainulindalë*. At the same time he demonstrates a classification that he has devised to show at what point individual motifs entered the story and whether or not they remained permanent features. By this means he shows how the subtle changes in Tolkien's expression between the different drafts increasingly ground the literary myth in Catholic theology.

Jason Fisher and Nils Ivar Agøy both concentrate on the important role played by Christopher Tolkien in the reception of the 'Silmarillion' tales through his decisions which cast the legendarium into an authoritative (though by no means final) form. For Jason Fisher, this is an achievement to be compared with those of St. Jerome and Elias Lönnrot. In the latter case the similarity is appropriate in view of the influence exercised by the Finnish language and its mythology on the young J. R. R. Tolkien, further examples of which are presented here. Nils Ivar Agøy examines the consequences for the narrative perspective of Christopher Tolkien's decision to omit any kind of frame narrative. In default, the reader has to fall back on hints from *The Lord of the Rings*, both in the main narrative and in the Prologue and Appendices, that *The Silmarillion* is identical with, or at least derived from, Bilbo's 'Translations from the Elvish'. However, closer investigation shows this to be unsustainable for the narrative as presented in the 1977 edition.

Philology, theology, mythography, narratology: these are just some of the approaches that have proved to be fruitful as *Silmarillion* criticism has grown up over the last thirty years. No doubt more will emerge now that Tolkien is increasingly accepted as a mainstream author. By its very nature *The Silmarillion* is unlikely ever to achieve a popularity anything like that of *The Lord of the Rings*, but since the mythological background lies at the heart of Tolkien's thought, critics will ignore it only at the risk of producing inaccurate and partial readings. It may not be to everyone's taste, but it is surely much harder nowadays to claim that the book is unreadable. It remains to be seen what changes in outlook the next thirty years may bring.

Allan Turner
Marburg, September 2007.

A Mythology for England

RHONA BEARE

Abstract

Tolkien regretted that England had no stories of its own, bound up with its tongue and soil and climate. It is possible to show by comparison with other, traditional tales that there exists a "North-western temper and temperature" quite different from the sensibility and motifs of Mediterranean or eastern cultures, which he set out to recapture in his writing. An important factor is climate, which has an effect on language and the myths recounted in it. The story of the silmarils is connected not only with the soil of England but with the language; Eärendil is derived from *earendel*, for which further new evidence is adduced to demonstrate that it refers to *lucifer*, Venus as morning star.

Scarcely anything remains of the pagan myths of the Angles and Saxons. Tolkien wanted to repair this loss by composing myths appropriate to England. Greek mythology is not appropriate, because it is influenced by the warm dry climate of Greece. England is cool, cloudy, misty and damp; Celtic lands have even more cloud, mist and rain. Celtic myths therefore, as Charles Squire pointed out, should appeal to the English more than Greek ones. Iceland is cloudy and misty, and chillier even than north Scotland. The Anglo-Saxons were Germanic, like the Scandinavians. If Woden was as like Odin as his name suggests, the myths were similar. England however is milder than Iceland; the pagan myths of England may have been less bleak than the Icelandic ones. William Morris loved the Icelandic sagas, but his best efforts do not achieve the Norse grimness. Linklater (1965: x) writes:

> In 1876 William Morris published a spirited narrative poem called Sigurd the Volsung [...] It does not convey the *sensation* of a legend [...] told, with a reticent

acceptance of great men's ineluctable doom, under the immensity of the Arctic night and a roof straining against the gale. It is all too easy, too genial in its acceptance of tragedy; it is Thames-side heroism, not the cold reality of Borgarness or Bergthorsknoll in the dark flat land that marches with the sea.

Bergthorsknoll was the home of Burnt Njal. On Borgarness (old name Digraness) is the howe in which Egil buried his father Skallagrim and his son Bodvar, as related in *Egil's Saga*. The authors of the two sagas knew these places; it is because they were Icelanders that their acceptance of tragedy was not "too genial". Linklater may mean that no Englishman living comfortably beside the Thames in 1876 could achieve the cold realism of Borgarness. Alternatively, if he thinks climate the cause, and England's climate unchanged since Anglo-Saxon times, Linklater may suppose that the English author of *Beowulf* could not achieve cold realism. But in the eighth century England contained great forests, marshes, wilderness. The uninhabited parts were not as wild as in Iceland, but they were dangerous enough. C.S. Lewis wrote to Arthur Greeves on 1st November 1916:

> If you are to enjoy *Beowulf*, you must [...] put yourself back in the position of the people for whom it was first made. When I was reading it I tried to imagine myself as an old Saxon thane sitting in my hall of a winter's night, with the wolves and storm outside and the old fellow singing his story. In this way you get the atmosphere of terror that runs through it – the horror of the old barbarous days when the land was all forests and when you thought that a demon might come to your house any night and carry you off. The description of Grendel stalking up from his 'fen and fastness' thrilled me.
> (Hooper, 1979: 143)

Tolkien would not say that *Beowulf*, or the poem of the battle of Maldon, was "too easy, too genial in its acceptance of tragedy". In 'Beowulf: the Monsters and the Critics' (1983a: 18f.) he talks of:

> the exaltation of undefeated will [...] this indomitability, this paradox of defeat inevitable yet unacknowledged [...] man at war with the hostile world, and his inevitable overthrow in time [...] It is the theme in its deadly seriousness that begets the dignity of tone [...] So deadly and ineluctable is the underlying thought [...] Death comes to the feast.

In the eighth century an English poet could see "cold reality" almost as clearly as an Icelander.

Since Tolkien wanted to compose a body of myth appropriate to England, he gave to Beleriand a maritime climate, very like England's. The Great Sea resembles the Atlantic. Because the sea is to the west, the west wind is mild and wet (*Silm* 119).[1] The north is cold, not only because we are in the northern hemisphere, but because Morgoth, who loves extremes, lives in the north. Winter can be severe (*Silm* 215), with heavy falls of snow, but summer is pleasant. There is no mention of drought, which suggests that the rainfall is like England's. The woods of Beleriand and its northern borders are of pine on Dorthonion, of birch in Nimbrethil, of oak and beech within the Girdle of Melian, of willow in Nan-tathren. Beleg's bow (p.208) is of yew. There are alders round Tarn Aeluin (*Silm* 163). All these trees are native to England.

Tolkien tells us (*Letters*, p.176) that the elves speak Sindarin, to which he has given "a linguistic character very like (though not identical with) British-Welsh". He finds this character attractive, and "it seems to fit the rather 'Celtic' type of legends and stories told of its speakers". The Noldor were self-exiled from paradise to Middle-earth. In the Irish tale *The Voyage of Saint Brendan*, the Neutral Angels, exiled from paradise to Middle-earth,

---

[1] By *Silm* 119, I mean p. 119 of *The Silmarillion*.

are sweet singers. The Tuatha de Danaan came from paradise to Middle-earth. When the Noldor land at Losgar (*Silm* 90), they burn their ships. So, according to Geoffrey Keating, did the Tuatha when they landed in Ireland.[2] When Beren tells Thingol that he wishes to marry Lúthien, Thingol sends him on a dangerous quest. Similarly in *The Mabinogion*, when Culhwch tells the giant that he wishes to marry Olwen, the giant sends him on a dangerous quest. In its legends, therefore, as well as in its climate, Beleriand is "redolent of our 'air' (the clime and soil of the North West)", as Tolkien says (*Letters*, p.144).

Because of its Mediterranean climate, vineyards and olive-groves flourish in Greece. Homer's heroes drink wine and anoint themselves with olive oil. A goddess anoints herself with oil after a bath (*Odyssey* 8.364), as men do (*Iliad* 10.577). Dionysus gave men the vine; Athena gave Athens the olive. In England, Iceland and the Celtic lands, beer and mead were the native drinks; wine was imported. In Beleriand the elves drink wine and mead. We are not told whether they imported the wine, or planted vineyards, as the monks did in England, for instance at Rochester.

Charles Squire (1905: 2-4) urged the English to read Welsh and Irish myths because the gods and heroes of the Celts were the natural inhabitants of the British landscape. The English had too long been content with the myths of the Greeks and Romans, though Greek gods and heroes are native to the Mediterranean lands, and foreign to the British landscape. In eighteenth-century English poetry every wood was a "grove" and every country lass a "nymph". At last Greek myth began to lose its power:

> Its potency became somewhat exhausted. Alien and exotic to English soil, it degenerated slowly into a convention [...] The Celtic mythology has little of the heavy crudeness that repels one in Teutonic and Scandinavian story. It is as beautiful and graceful as the

---

[2] Keating lived c. 1570 - c. 1650. He wrote a *History of Ireland* in Irish, which has been edited with translation and notes by David Comyn (London, 1902). For the Tuatha, see Vol. 1, p.215. [Also available online at <ftp:///.ucc.ie/pub/celt/texts/T100054.sgml>.]

> Greek; and, unlike the Greek, which is a reflection of a clime and soil which few of us will ever see, it is our own. Divinities should, surely, seem the inevitable outgrowth of the land they move in! How strange Apollo would appear, naked among icebergs, or fur-clad Thor striding under groves of palms! The Celtic gods and heroes are the natural inhabitants of a British landscape, not seeming foreign and out-of-place in a scene where there is no vine or olive, but 'shading in with' our homely oak and bracken, gorse and heath.

It is not from Greek poets that we learned to picture Apollo naked. After Greek sculptors had learned to carve nude athletes, Phidias carved worthy images of the nude Apollo, and such statues have accustomed us to thinking that the god himself rarely wore clothes. Centuries after Phidias, and in Italy, Michelangelo carved godlike nudes. No Phidias or Michelangelo could have been born in England. Pevsner (1956: 120) says "The English are not a sculptural nation", and also "The English have nothing of the Italian, the Mediterranean confidence in the body" (p. 122). Pevsner attributes this, like all English characteristics, to England's cooler, mistier climate. Kenneth Clark (1960) says in Chapter 2 that the nude Apollo arose naturally from the Greek culture, and could not have arisen in England. In Chapter 1 he writes:

> Only in countries touching on the Mediterranean has the nude been at home; and even there its meaning was often forgotten. [...] When nude figures which had been evolved to express an idea ceased to do so, and were represented for their physical perfection alone, they lost their value. This was the fatal legacy of neo-classicism... The academic nudes of the nineteenth century are lifeless because they no longer embodied real human needs and experiences.
> (Clark, 1960: 7-8, 22)

Charles Squire was right. Phidias' Apollo was the "inevitable outgrowth" of ancient Greece; he reflected that clime, soil and culture. The strong sunlight, the olive groves, the naked athletes gleaming with oil, the Olympic and Pythian Games, these are his natural background and account for his nudity. Squire said that the Celtic gods and heroes, who would be out of place in Greece, shade in with the English oak and bracken. In the same sense, Thingol's subjects shaded in with the woods of Doriath: the beeches of Neldoreth and the oaks of Nivrim (*Silm* 121-2). Greenwood the Great (later called Mirkwood) contained oak and beech (*Silm* 299). In *The Lord of the Rings*, 'The Council of Elrond', Legolas of Northern Mirkwood is described as "a strange Elf clad in green and brown": protective colouring. The elves of Lórien were camouflaged by the cloaks which they wore; they gave them to the Company in 'Farewell to Lórien':

> It was hard to say of what colour they were: grey with the hue of twilight under the trees they seemed to be; and yet if they were moved, or set in another light, they were green as shadowed leaves, or brown as fallow fields by night, dusk-silver as water under stars.

The elves do not wear these cloaks solely as camouflage, but also because the cloaks are the colour of the things they love: "leaf and branch, water and stone [...] under the twilight of Lórien that we love; for we put the thought of all that we love into all that we make". As Sam Gamgee says (in 'The Mirror of Galadriel'), "They seem to belong here, more even than Hobbits do in the Shire. Whether they've made the land, or the land's made them, it's hard to say".

The Green Elves were beautiful and sang beautifully. They were elusive, for their clothes were the colour of leaves (*Silm* 96). They lived in Ossiriand (*Silm* 123):

> The woodcraft of the Elves of Ossiriand was such that a stranger might pass through their land from end to end and see none of them. They were clad in green in spring and summer, and the sound of their singing could be heard even across the waters of Gelion; wherefore the Noldor named that country Lindon, the land of music.

We see here "the fair elusive beauty that some call Celtic", which Tolkien hoped to achieve (*Letters*, p.144). The supreme example of it is Lúthien. She was "the fairest of the Children of Ilúvatar that was or ever shall be" (*Silm* 56). She eluded Beren (p.165); she escaped from her father (p.172) and from Nargothrond (p.175). She eluded Sauron (p.175) by casting her dark cloak before his eyes. She disguised herself in the skin of a vampire bat (p.179), which enabled her to fly. She offered to sing to Morgoth (p.180): "She eluded his sight, and out of the shadows began a song of such surpassing loveliness [...] that he listened perforce; and a blindness came upon him." All his attendants fell asleep (p.181): "Then Lúthien catching up her winged robe sprang into the air, and her voice came dropping down like rain into pools, profound and dark. She cast her cloak before his eyes, and set upon him a dream".

With her black hair and dark cloak and dark bat-skin, Lúthien resembles Yeats' queen of the little people (fairies):[3]

> A very beautiful tall woman came out of the cave. I had [...] fallen into a kind of trance, in which what we call the unreal had begun to take upon itself a masterful reality, and was able to see the faint gleam of golden ornaments, the shadowy blossom of dim hair [...] Tall, glimmering queen, come near.

Lúthien also resembles the "glimmering girl" who can disappear or turn into a fish in Yeats' 'Song of the Wandering Aengus': she eludes Aengus and he searches for her as Beren searched for the elusive Lúthien.

In 1937 Tolkien sent to his publishers the *Lay of Leithian* and the *Quenta Silmarillion*. The publishers submitted to their reader Edward Crankshaw the Lay (which is about Beren and Lúthien) and the corresponding chapter of the Quenta. Crankshaw mistook Beren and Lúthien for characters in an early Celtic Geste (Tolkien, 1985: 364-5). He mistook

---

[3] In the chapter called 'Regina, Regina Pigmeorum, Veni' in *The Celtic Twilight*, first published 1893.

the *Silmarillion* chapter for a prose translation of the Geste by some modern writer, who had also put it into verse, producing the Lay. The reader much preferred the prose, but found the names 'eye-splitting'. In his report to the publishers Crankshaw said that the prose version "has something of that mad, bright-eyed beauty that perplexes all Anglo-Saxons in face of Celtic art".

These comments were passed on to Tolkien, who replied to the publishers (*Letters*, p.26) that the names and the tales were not Celtic (that is, Tolkien had invented them, not translated them from a Celtic language). Tolkien agreed that (some) Celtic tales were mad (that is, incoherent and self-contradictory), but denied that he himself was. Since the tale of Beren and Lúthien is coherent and consistent, but (like many Celtic tales) contains frequent shape-changing and much magic, it may have been the magic that struck Crankshaw as mad. If so, Tolkien would not understand, for he did not realise that Crankshaw had only read the chapter on Beren and Lúthien, which contains far more magic than the stories of Túrin and of Tuor. When he refers to the rejection of the Quenta (*Letters*, pp.113, 136, 215), he says that the publishers' reader allowed it a certain beauty, but of a Celtic kind "irritating" (or "intolerable" or "maddening") to Anglo-Saxons (at least in large doses).

Charlotte and Denis Plimmer, apparently quoting Tolkien, said the reader had turned the Quenta down as being "too dark and Celtic for modern Anglo-Saxons". Tolkien hopes (*Letters*, p.374) that that was not what the reader objected to, since after revision (which he admits it needed) it "retains the character thus misdescribed". He may mean that *The Silmarillion* is still dark and tragic, but the darkness is Anglo-Saxon, not Celtic. See 'English and Welsh' (Tolkien, 1983a: 172); Tolkien did not accept the view that the Saxon is practical, and the Celt is "full of vague and misty imaginations". At the beginning of *The Mabinogion*, when Pwyll meets Arawn, Pwyll shows himself "a very practical man, with a feeling for bright colour". He is practical, but ill-mannered, when he drives Arawn's pack away from the stag they have killed and baits his own pack on it. He shows his feeling for bright colour when he notices that Arawn's hounds are white with red ears (which proves them otherworldly). If you wanted a "vague and misty" account of this meeting, you would have to go to an Anglo-Saxon poet; his account would have no colour words, and the half-seen hounds would be "huge shadows pursuing shadows to the brink of a bottomless pool". *Beowulf* is "full of dark and twilight, and laden with sorrow and regret".

Since Arawn is a hunter and a prince of Annwn, Tolkien must associate him with the hunter Oromë, whose Sindarin name is Araw (*Silm* 345) and who comes from Annûn (*Silm* 355). Tolkien regards Arawn as King of the Dead.

The elves who are camouflaged by their clothes are Wood-elves and love trees. So did Tolkien. He tells us that even in childhood the thing he liked best in Red Indian tales was the forests. (This is in 'On Fairy-stories', Tolkien 1983a: 134.) In *The Lord of the Rings*, the Golden Wood of Lórien is contrasted with Fangorn, and Fangorn with Mirkwood. In *Silm* 298, Lórien is the "hidden land" between two rivers "where the trees bore flowers of gold and no orc or evil thing dared ever come". In *Silm* 155 there is a sinister forest:

> It was called [...] Taur-nu-Fuin, The Forest under Nightshade. The trees that grew there [...] were black and grim, and their roots were tangled, groping in the dark like claws. Those who strayed among them became lost and blind, and were strangled or pursued to madness by phantoms of terror.

Greenwood the Great (*Silm* 299) had once belonged to the elves, but a change came:

> A darkness crept slowly through the wood from the southward, and fear walked there in shadowy glades; fell beasts came hunting, and cruel and evil creatures laid there their snares. Then the name of the forest was changed and Mirkwood it was called, for the nightshade lay deep there, and few dared to pass through.

Mirkwood's name links it to Germanic myth. In *Letters*, p.369, Tolkien writes:

> Mirkwood is not an invention of mine, but a very ancient name, weighted with legendary associations. It was probably the Primitive Germanic name for the great mountainous forest regions that anciently formed a barrier to the south of the lands of Germanic expansion. In some traditions it became used especially of the boundary between Goths and Huns.

There were forests in central Germany as well. Caesar (*Gallic War*, 6.25-28) describes the Hercynian Forest, sixty days' journey in length and nine in width; it contains animals not found elsewhere, such as a one-horned reindeer, and the aurochs, a giant ox which cannot be tamed.

These forests hampered the Roman army. Varus was marching between treacherous swamps and impenetrable forest when he was ambushed by Arminius. In the earliest times the Germanic peoples had learned to fear the forests, and their descendants (in Germany and in Saxon England) inherited the phobia. It is reflected in their tales and their visual arts. Kenneth Clark, in *Landscape into Art*, Chapter 3, which he calls 'Landscape of Fantasy', discusses the influence of this phobia on painting and poetry. It made northern art different from Greek and Roman art, for deforestation began early in Greece, and by Tacitus' day Italy had vineyards and sheep where there had once been trees, whereas Germany "bristles with forests or reeks with fens" (Tacitus, *Germania* 5.1)[4]. The old fear of the forests shows itself in Grünewald and Bosch, making them "expressionist" artists like Van Gogh:

> Expressionist art is fundamentally a northern and an anti-classical form, and prolongs, both in its imagery and its complex rhythms, the restless, organic art of the folk-

---

[4] Tacitus, *Germania*, translated with commentary by J. B. Rives, Oxford: Clarendon Press, 1999.

wandering period. It is forest born, and even when it does not actually represent fir trees and undergrowth – as in German painting it almost invariably does – their gnarled and shaggy forms dominate the design. The last symbol of these old German obsessive fears, tamed and domesticated by a century of materialism, is the Christmas tree. The first, or one of the first, is to be found in *Beowulf*, in the passage describing Grendel's Mere, and it is worth quoting, as it contains almost all elements of which the landscape of fantasy is composed.
(Clark, 1961: 50)

Clark then quotes the lines (1345-1372) in which Hrothgar tells Beowulf that Grendel has a female companion. They have been glimpsed in a lonely district near a hellish mere above which hangs a wood "fast-rooted", clinging by its roots, and over-shadowing the mere. This wood made such an impression on Tolkien that he drew two pictures of the mere and the fast-rooted trees (reproduced in Hammond & Scull, 1995: 53-55).

The *Beowulf*-poet goes on to say that a hart pursued by the hounds would rather be killed than escape by plunging in, because the mere is so hellish. Apparently to plunge in is to go straight to hell. There is a story of a Cornish priest called Dando, too fond of hunting. The devil, in the form of a mounted huntsman, seized Dando and plunged into a stream, followed by the hounds.[5] In some versions of the Wild Hunt it is the devil who is the Wild Huntsman; in other versions it is Odin. It is possible that at the start of *The Mabinogion* Arawn, a king from the other world, is the Wild Huntsman. The colour of his hounds (white with red ears) proves that they are other-worldly. Tolkien says in 'English and Welsh' that the Anglo-Saxon poet would have made such a hunt more eerie. The hounds would not be brightly coloured:

> It is easy to imagine how he would have managed it: ominous, colourless, with the wind blowing and a *wóma* in the distance, as the half-seen hounds came baying in

---

[5] *Funk and Wagnall's Dictionary of Folklore* under WILD HUNT.

the gloom, huge shadows pursuing shadows to the brink of a bottomless pool.

Tolkien's bottomless pool is modelled on Grendel's Mere, whose depth, says Hrothgar, no one knows. Wind is connected with *wóma*. *Wóma* means a rush or noise; it can be the rushing sound made by the wind, or by the Icelandic god Omi, whom the English would call Wóma. He is the god of the wind and air. Grimm writes:[6] "We may imagine *Omi, Wóma* as an air-god, like the Hindu Indras, whose rush is heard in the sky at the break of day, in the din of battle, and the tramp of the 'furious host'".

The Furious Host is the Wild Hunt. In Old English daybreak can be called day-red and day-red-*wóma*. The sounds Tolkien associates with daybreak are the dawn wind rustling in the trees; cockcrow or birdsong; the blast of horns and trumpets. Day-red suggests a scarlet sunrise; and scarlet, by synaesthesia, suggests a trumpet blast. Compare the description of Oromë the hunter, *Silm* 29: the sound of his horn "is like the upgoing of the Sun in scarlet". He is good, and hunts evil creatures; but the elves had stories of "the dark Rider upon his wild horse that pursued those that wandered to take them and devour them" (*Silm* 50). This suggests the Wild Hunt led by the devil. The Wild Hunt belongs to the folk-lore of North West Europe; it is not found in the myths of Greece and Rome.

Climate makes the Frenchmen of Paris different from the Bretons; it explains why the fairy-tales of Perrault (courtly and sophisticated) are so unlike Breton tales. Sunny France makes the French clear-thinking, sensible, sane; cloud and mist give the Bretons imagination and the feeling for romanticism. The French, including Perrault, do not believe in fairies; the Bretons take the Other World seriously. Dutton and Holden (1946:3) say:

> The climate of a country directly affects the characteristics of the inhabitants. The French are hard-working and clear-thinking; the bracing air makes them strong and energetic; and stimulates them mentally to a

---

[6] Jacob Grimm, *Teutonic Mythology*, trans. Stallybrass (London, 1882-8), Vol.1 p.145.

highly developed standard of common sense. This excellent quality is, indeed, sometimes carried to extreme lengths, and, except amongst those with Celtic blood, one often misses in this highly sane outlook the imagination and feeling for romanticism which is to be found amongst the inhabitants of cloudy countries.

In 'Beowulf: the Monsters and the Critics' Tolkien tells us how the Greek myths differ from the Icelandic ones. The bleak climate of the North has inspired a bleak but noble philosophy. Brave men are the allies of the gods in a long war against giants, monsters and the powers of darkness. The war will end in the defeat and death of the gods and their allies, but this prospect does not dismay them. The Greeks and Romans, by contrast, believed that the Olympian gods had long ago defeated the titans and giants, and now had nothing to fear. Men were not the allies of the gods in a war against monsters; indeed, some monsters (such as Vulcan's son Cacus) were the children of Olympian gods. The man-eating Cyclops was a son of Poseidon, who punished Odysseus for blinding him.

It is not clear in Aeschylus' *Prometheus Bound* that Zeus is in the right and the titans in the wrong; Shelley thought Zeus a tyrant. It is not clear that Odin is more honest than the Frost-giants. In Tolkien's *Silmarillion* it is obvious that Morgoth and the orcs are in the wrong and are wicked. Tolkien is not a dualist; there is only one ultimate reality, the One, who is good, and who created Morgoth himself capable of being good. C.S. Lewis discusses Norse dualism in 'Evil and Good':

> Dualism can be a manly creed. In the Norse form ('The giants will beat the gods in the end, but I am on the side of the gods') it is nobler by many degrees than most philosophies of the moment. But it is only a half-way house.
> (Lewis, 2000: 95)

In *The Silmarillion* the elves correspond to the Norse gods; good men are their allies in a long war against Morgoth. The elves can be killed or maimed. The elf Maedhros lost a hand; so did the Norse god Tyr. Morgoth is bound to defeat the elves in the end, because he is stronger, and because of the Doom of the Noldor. Only the Valar, who are his equals, can defeat Morgoth. Morgoth's victories over the elves remind us of Ragnarök, in which the gods are killed by the monsters.

The Icelandic myth of Ragnarök inspired men to fight to the last around their fallen chief, and to tell stories of such fights. Since there are similar stories in Old English, Tolkien believes that the pagan Angles and Saxons had a myth of the Ragnarök type. The myth gave them Northern courage; when they lost hope, they did not lose heart. We see this courage in *The Silmarillion*, in the last stand of the Men of Dorlómin (p.194) and in Húrin's defiance of Morgoth (pp.186-7). This is heroism.

The greatest hero of the north was Sigurd (Siegfried), and his greatest deed was to kill the dragon Fáfnir. The treasure that he won eventually caused his death. The most heroic of the gods was Thor, who at Ragnarök kills the World Serpent and dies of its poison. We can compare Beowulf, who killed a dragon and died of poisoned wounds. In *Silm* 193 Glaurung and a dwarf-lord wound each other, but only the dwarf dies; Túrin kills Glaurung (p.222), but the dying dragon's words to Níniel lead to her suicide and Túrin's.

Fáfnir when dying talks with Sigurd; Glaurung dying talks to Níniel (*Silm* 223); in *The Hobbit*, Smaug talks with Bilbo. A dragon's words are poisonous; a man whose words are poisonous is called Wormtongue. Fáfnir warns Sigurd that if he takes the treasure other men will covet it; Glaurung tells Níniel that she has married her brother; Smaug poisons Bilbo's mind against the dwarves. In *Letters*, p.134, Tolkien writes:

> I find dragons a fascinating product of imagination. But I don't think the Beowulf one is frightfully good. But the whole problem of the intrusion of the dragon into northern imagination and its transformation there is one I do not know enough about. Fáfnir in the late Norse

versions of the Sigurd story is better; and Smaug and his conversation obviously is in debt there.

By "intrusion" he means that southerners had stories of dragons (or giant serpents) before the Saxons and Scandinavians did. In Greek myth, dragons are not like Fáfnir. Cadmus' dragon guarded a spring of water. Others guard a treasure that is not man-made: it is the Golden Fleece, or a tree bearing golden apples. They are not avaricious; they are like watch-dogs, guarding someone else's property. Dragons greedy for treasure are northern. Like vikings, they desire objects made by man and of gold: cups, bowls, rings and crowns. Sigurd talks in riddles to Fáfnir; Bilbo talks in riddles to Smaug. In Greek myth, Oedipus talks with the Sphinx and solves the riddle, but Cadmus does not talk with the dragon. In Greek myth there are fire-breathing bulls, but no fire-breathing serpents.

In *Letters*, p. 212 Tolkien writes: "It has always been with me [...] the deep response to legends [...] that have [...] the Northwestern temper and temperature". To what legends did Tolkien "always" respond? Certainly to the story of Sigurd and Fáfnir, which he read as a child in Andrew Lang's *Red Fairy Book*. In some other book he apparently found a green dragon and liked the colour, for he tells us (*Letters*, p.214) that at about the age of seven he tried to write a story about "a green great dragon". Later in life he wrote a poem on a green dragon, and painted a picture of one. He probably read that Ouroboros, the dragon of the alchemists that symbolizes eternity, is green. Claudian in 400 AD (*On Stilicho's Consulship*, 2.424-432) said that the serpent of eternity, which swallows its own tail, has green scales. This serpent or dragon holds its tail in its mouth in order to form itself into a circle, which is endless, like eternity. Some say Ouroboros "bites" its tail, others that it "eats" it. The Latin for Tail-biter would be Caudimordax. In *Farmer Giles of Ham*, Tolkien (as a joke) gives this name not to the dragon but to the sword. It seems that Chrysophylax was green. Two of Pauline Baynes' pictures of Chrysophylax have been used on cover designs, with the dragon coloured green (Tolkien, 1975 and 1983b). In *The Silmarillion*, Ancalagon is called "the Black" on p.252, and Glaurung's name shows that he is golden, like Smaug. The Anglo-Saxons and Icelanders were less interested in this than Tolkien; they did not tell us the colour of Beowulf's dragon or of Fáfnir.

Tolkien did not think Beowulf's dragon as good as Sigurd's, which was a proper fairy-story dragon, whereas Beowulf's was little more than a personification of dragonishness. In 'Beowulf: the Monsters and the Critics' he writes:

> Beowulf's dragon, if one wishes to criticize, is not to be blamed for being a dragon, but rather for not being dragon enough, plain pure fairy-story dragon. There are in the poem some vivid touches of the right kind – as *þa se wyrm onwoc, wroht wæs geniwad; stonc æfter stane*, 2285.
> (Tolkien, 1983a: 17)

Tolkien means lines 2287-8. Someone has stolen a gold cup from the dragon; the dragon awakes, and discovers the theft. Tolkien did not tell us what he thinks *stonc* means. Many say it means 'moved quickly'. In the Penguin translation Michael Alexander turns this into 'glided': "The waking of the worm awoke the feud: he glided along the rock". In my opinion Tolkien took *stonc* to mean 'sniffed, followed the scent'. In *The Hobbit*, when Bilbo had stolen Smaug's gold cup and fled, Smaug "stirred and stretched forth his neck to sniff". (After writing this I went to the Bodleian and looked at the manuscript of Tolkien's translation of *Beowulf*. It is copyright and I am forbidden to quote even one word; but after consulting it I had no need to alter what is written above.) For other "vivid touches of the right kind", see Michael Drout's edition of *Beowulf and the Critics* (2002: 109), where Tolkien gives lines 2293ff as an example. Michael Alexander translates:

> The treasure-guard eagerly
> quartered the ground to discover the man
> who had done him wrong during his sleep.

> Seething with rage, he circled the barrow's
> whole outer wall.

These vivid touches are what Tolkien had in mind when he wrote:

> There are in the poem some vivid touches of the right kind [...] in which this dragon is real worm, with a bestial life and thought of his own, but the conception, none the less, approaches *draconitas* rather than *draco*: a personification of malice, greed, destruction (the evil side of heroic life), and of the undiscriminating cruelty of fortune that distinguishes not good or bad (the evil aspect of all life). But for *Beowulf*, the poem, that is as it should be. In this poem the balance is nice, but it is preserved. The large symbolism is near the surface, but it does not break through, nor become allegory.
> (Tolkien:1983a: 17)

Beowulf and the dragon, Sigurd and the dragon: these stories have "the north-western temper and temperature". Tolkien loved them as soon as he met them. But there are other legends that a man's heart might remember even before he read or heard of them – provided that he and his ancestors lived in the North West. In *Letters*, p.212, Tolkien says this is true of the legend that Atlantis was destroyed by a great wave, but some Atlanteans sailed to Middle-earth as culture-heroes. They are the Men out of the Sea, men like Sheaf who in English legend arrived as a child asleep in a boat. The Swan Knight also arrived asleep in a boat. An Englishman may inherit this race-memory:

> His heart may remember, even if he has been cut off from all oral tradition, the rumour all along the coasts of the Men out of the Sea. I say this about the 'heart', for I have what some might call an Atlantis complex. Possibly inherited ... Inherited from me (I suppose) by only one of my children. I mean the terrible recurrent dream (beginning with memory) of the great Wave, towering

up, and coming in ineluctably over the trees and green fields.

Sheaf, or Shield Sheafing, is shown by his name to be a culture-hero teaching men how to grow corn. The corn-hero is likely to have begun as a corn-god, a dying god, arriving by boat every spring, and sailing away in a funeral boat every autumn. Sheaf came, according to Baring-Gould (1967: 588, 601), like the Swan Knight, from the paradise in the western sea that some call Avalon and Plato calls Atlantis. Tolkien says Sheaf was not the only culture-hero (*Letters*, p.347). Arthur may count as a culture-hero. Balder may have been a culture-hero or a dying god. The Swan Knight sailed back home. Arthur sailed off to Avalon, dying but hoping to be healed; the Bretons say he will return. Balder was given ship-burial, and will one day return. Shield Sheafing sailed off in a funeral boat, but is not actually said to have died. Tolkien turns them into Númenoreans, visiting Middle-earth to help and teach (*Silm* 263): "Corn and wine they brought, and they instructed Men in the sowing of seed and the grinding of grain, in the hewing of wood and the shaping of stone." Compare Tolkien's retelling of the story of King Sheaf (*Lost Road*, 85).

Tolkien connected his dream of the Great Wave with the drowning of Atlantis. North West Europe has its flood-legends. In Cardigan Bay the sea covers the lost Cantrevs of Dyfed; the Land of Lyonesse once stretched from Cornwall to the Scilly Isles; the city of Ys once stood on the coast of Brittany. The Drysidae (perhaps Druids) said that some of the ancestors of the Gauls came "from very distant islands and from regions across the Rhine, driven from their homes by frequent wars and by the inundation of the raging sea" (my translation); so wrote the historian Timagenes, quoted by Ammianus Marcellinus, 15.9.4. If the islands were inundated, that would be like the drowning of Atlantis. Though Plato was a Greek, and said Solon learned the tale of Atlantis in Egypt, there are enough floods and culture heroes (Men of the Sea) in the legends of North West Europe to persuade Tolkien that his Great Wave was a racial memory belonging to the North

West. We recognize the wave of his dream in *Silm* 279: "the mounting wave, green and cold and plumed with foam, climbing over the land".

We need not be surprised to find in the Akallabêth elements that do not come from the North West. Tolkien tells us (*Letters*, p. 144) that he found "as an ingredient" in the legends of other lands things of the quality that he sought. He found in Plato the downfall of imperialist Atlantis, in China the story that the First Emperor (who died in 210 BC) longed to escape death by finding the elixir of life or the Islands of the Immortals. Tolkien's Númenoreans, like the First Emperor, tried to lengthen their lives (*Silm* 266). Sauron told Ar-Pharazôn that if he broke a taboo he would become immortal; the serpent told Eve that if she broke a taboo she would become like God, knowing good and evil. The Irish said that the first invasion of Ireland was led by Noah's niece, forty days before the Flood. Tolkien assimilated the drowning of Númenor to Noah's Flood, and Elendil to Noah. Elendil is "a Noachian figure" (*Letters*, p. 156) and his followers are "in a kind of Noachian situation" (*Letters*, p. 206). He also resembles Aeneas, escaping from burning Troy to Italy. Aeneas was the son of Venus, and there was a story that the planet Venus guided Aeneas to Italy; Conington, in his edition of the *Aeneid*, mentions it in his note on *Aen.* 2.801. Similarly the first settlers in Númenor were guided there by the Star of Eärendil. The Star is the evening star (Venus), and Eärendil is the father of Númenor's first king. Venus is evening star when it sets in the West after the sun; it is morning star when it rises in the east before the sun. In *The Silmarillion* p. 250 the Star of Eärendil is "seen at morning or at evening, glimmering in sunrise or sunset". It is not just a planet; it is the ship in which Eärendil sails with the silmaril on his brow. Therefore it can do things Venus does not do, as in *Silm* 252 where for twenty four hours Eärendil and the eagles fight dragons in the sky above Thangorodrim. At midnight Eärendil must have been at the zenith.

For the evening star directly overhead at midnight, compare Milton's *Comus* 93-94. At midnight Comus says to his drunken followers: "The star that bids the shepherd fold / Now the top of heaven doth hold". As editors point out, it is the evening star that bids the shepherd take his flock to the fold. The editors do not point out that Comus imagines the Star as *rising* in the west at sunset, and continuing to rise till midnight. Roman poets also talk of the evening star as rising. Tolkien does so *Silm* 250; also in *The Lord of the Rings*, as Galadriel leads Frodo and Sam into her garden. The Roman poets may merely mean that the evening star *appears* in the west after sunset; to myth-makers the star literally rises in the west. Venus actually is overhead at midday, but we do not see it; what we do not see is irrelevant to myth. Tolkien therefore never says that Eärendil habitually rises in the east, crosses the sky (a little before or after the sun), and sets in the west. Instead, Tolkien says that Eärendil glimmers in sunrise or sunset.

Myths leave traces on language. Since the pagan myths had been lost, Tolkien looked for the traces they had left on Old English. He found a trace in the word *earendel, eorendel*.[7] The English word is a noun, but may originally have been a personal name, as are the related forms in other Germanic languages. For instance, Orendel is the hero of a German epic. Auriwandalo is a man's name used among the Lombards. In Icelandic Aurvandill is the name not of an ordinary man, but of a friend of Thor, whose frostbitten toe was turned by Thor into the Star called Aurvandill's Toe.[8] There may have been a pagan myth about a hero called Earendel, who became the morning star.

Glosses throw some light on the meaning of the noun *earendel* in OE. In a collection of Latin hymns with inter-linear glosses, *earendel* is used to translate *aurora* 'dawn'; in the Épinal glossary, *earendel* and *leoma* are used to translate *iubar* 'ray, radiance'.[9] *Iubar* properly means the first light of day, but can be used of radiance in general, e.g. the rays of the sun.

---

[7] See *Letters*, p. 385, and *Sauron* Defeated, pp. 301, 307-8.

[8] Snorri, Prose Edda, The Poesy of the Scalds, Ch. XVII. It has been suggested that this Star is Rigel, the bright star in Orion's left foot; see An Icelandic Dictionary, by Cleasby, Vigfusson and Craigie, under STJARNA. If Aurvandill's Toe is Rigel, Aurvandill may originally have been the constellation Orion.

[9] Cf. Stevenson (1851:16 and 30); Pheifer (1974), line 554; Sweet (1885).

Tolkien was more interested in the use of the word *earendel* in *Crist* 104 and in the *Blickling Homilies*; this is homily XIV (Morris 1880:163), which is on the Nativity of John the Baptist. According to Tolkien, in *Crist* and the homily *earendel* means the morning star, which is the planet Venus when it rises before the sun.

The Baptist's nativity is celebrated on 24 June, his martyrdom on 29 August. The Blickling homily on his nativity in some ways resembles the entry for 24 June in a martyrology written between 850 and 900 (Herzfeld 1900:102-5), which says:

> On the twenty-fourth day of the month is the birth of St. John the Baptist. He was born six months before Christ, and the archangel Gabriel announced his birth and told his father his name before he was born. This John was greater than any other man except Christ; all the patriarchs and prophets of God he surpasses, and all the apostles and martyrs he precedes and all those who were born from man and woman. He came into the world before Christ, as the morning star [*morgensteorra*] comes before the sun, as the herald [*bydel*] comes before the judge, and as the trumpet sounds before the king. John was the angel who went before God, because God wanted to go forth after six months in human form. John rejoiced in his mother's womb, when St. Mary came in to his mother Elizabeth; thereby he betokened that Christ had come into the womb of the pure woman. That was a quick messenger who tried to tell his message before he lived. No man is capable to explain the power of John the born angel.

The Blickling homily says John is the new *earendel* (morning star according to Tolkien); the Martyrology says John came before Christ as the morning star comes before the sun. Ælfric (homily 25 lines 96-100) says of the Baptist: "He was sent before the Lord, as the daystar (*dægsteorra*) goes before the sun; as the herald (*bydel*) goes before the judge; as the old covenant goes before the new one" (Clemoes 1997; my translation).

The Baptist is called an angel because he was God's messenger; the AV has "messenger" in Malachi 3.1 and Mark 1.2, but the Vulgate has *angelus*. Mark, quoting Malachi, represents God as saying to Christ: "I send my messenger [angel] before thy face, which shall prepare thy way before thee".

In Latin the morning star can be called *lucifer*. Bede (*Epist. Cath.* 128)[10] says that lucifer is the same planet as the evening star; because lucifer rises before the sun it can symbolize the Baptist who came before Christ. In Bede's hymn on the Baptist[11] the last verse goes: "Behold, says God, I send an angel to prepare your way and go before you as [...] lucifer goes before the sun".

There is a similar, but not identical, image in the anonymous Latin commentary, *Opus imperfectum in Matthaeum* (fifth century), once thought to be a translation of a work by Chrysostom. This says that Christ first appeared in public at his baptism, while John was still preaching, and the crowds turned from John to Christ; similarly the light first appears while lucifer the morning star is still rising, and causes it to fade.[12] Light here must mean daylight, dawn or the sun; it resembles Christ, who is the true light.

In Greek, the Baptist is compared to *heosphoros* 'dawn-bringer' (morning star) because he is the precursor of Christ as sun. See the sermons of Pseudo-Chrysostom on the Baptist (*PG* 50.791 and 61.760). The earliest Greek example (third century) is in Origen's commentary on the fourth gospel; see Lampe (1968) under *heosphoros*.

Ælfric said the Baptist went before Christ "as the herald goes before the judge; as the old covenant goes before the new". Compare a Pseudo-Augustine sermon:[13] "John is sent before Jesus Christ, as the old covenant

---

[10] Migne, Patrologia Latina (PL) 93.128.
[11] PL 94.628, hymn viii, for the Nativity of John the Baptist; my translation.
[12] Migne, Patrologia Graeca (PG) 56.657
[13] No. 196 §3 (PL 39.2111).

before the new [...] So the lamp is sent before the sun, the servant before the Lord, the friend before the bridegroom, the herald before the judge".

In *Blickling Homilies* 162 the Baptist is the herald (or crier) before the judge, but the OE word is *fricca*, not *bydel*. The Baptist is the angel who goes before the Lord. The Martyrology called the Baptist *morgensteorra*, Ælfric called him *dægsteorra*, but the Blickling homilist calls him the new *earendel*. Since Christ will be born in six months, it is high time for John to be born:

> And now the birth of Christ was at his appearing, and the new [*earendel*] was John the Baptist. And now the gleam [*leoma*] of the true Sun, God himself, shall come; let the crier give out his voice. And because that the Lord Christ is now the Judge, Saint John will be the trumpet and will therefore come with God himself upon this earth; let the [angel] go before him.[14]

A large part of this homily is based on a Latin sermon which calls the Baptist the new lucifer, and calls Christ the ray (*iubar*) of the true sun.[15] The relevant passage runs (in my translation):

> If John is going to come forth, let him now be born, for the birth of Christ is at hand; let the new lucifer rise, for the ray of the true sun bursts forth; let the herald cry out, for the judge is at hand; let the trumpet sound, for the king comes; and because God is about to come forth, let the angel now go ahead of him.

---

[14] The translation is taken from Morris (1880). Morris actually wrote "the new dayspring (or dawn)", but since I disagree with his interpretation I have kept the Old English word. Similarly, where Morris renders the Old English word engel as "messenger i.e. Saint John", I have substituted a more literal translation.

[15] This sermon is no. 199 of the Pseudo-Augustine sermons, PL 39.2117, and is no. 91 of the collected sermons of Petrus Chrysologus, PL 52.457B. That the homily was based on this sermon was known in 1940 to A. E. H. Swaen; see his article 'Notes on the Blickling Homiles' in *Neophilologus* Vol. xxv p. 269. Presumably it was also known to Tolkien.

Since *lucifer* is the Latin for morning star, that is what the Blickling homilist means by *earendel*. What Latin word lies behind *earendel* in *Crist* 104?

Crist 104 is the beginning of a lyric on Christ's Advent. Apart from the invocation of *earendel* and the sun's *leoma*, this lyric does not remind us of the Blickling homily; but it does remind us of the nativity of the Baptist, since it echoes Luke 1.78-79, words uttered by the Baptist's father a week after his birth. Through God's mercy, said the father, the 'rising' from on high has visited us, to illumine those who sit in darkness and in the shadow of death. The Vulgate uses *oriens* for 'rising': *uisitauit nos oriens ex alto, inluminare his qui in tenebris et in umbra mortis sedent*. The Greek word translated *oriens* is *anatolē*. *Oriens* is a participle, *anatolē* a noun. When they refer to a heavenly body, it is always the sun, unless some other heavenly body has been mentioned. *Anatolē* therefore means the rising of the sun, and *oriens* means *oriens sol*.[16]

Crist, after invoking *earendel* and the sun's *leoma*, continues:

> You by your own self continually illumine every hour. If you, God long since begotten of God, Son of the true Father, ever existed without beginning in the glory of heaven, then with confidence your own creation prays to you now on account of its needs, that you send us that bright sun, and yourself come so that you may illumine those who, shrouded in murk and in darkness, have already long continued here in endless night; enveloped in sins they have had to endure the dark shadow of death [...]
> (Bradley, 1982: 208)

Christ's titles include *uerus sol* 'true sun'; and (taken from Malachi 4.2) *sol iustitiae*, the sun of justice or righteousness that will arise with healing in his

---

[16] They cannot mean the rising of the morning star. They never mean the rising of the early dawn. See *Thesaurus Linguae Latinae*, col. 1005, lines 9-23. In Luke 1.78 the Authorised Version translates 'dayspring', a poetical word for daybreak, but this, since it can mean the period immediately before sunrise, is less precise and accurate than 'sunrise'. The New Jerusalem Bible in Luke 1.78 has 'the rising sun'.

wings. When Christ sends us "that bright sun", he comes himself; he is the *oriens sol* that illumines those who sit in darkness. There is an Advent antiphon on this subject: "O Oriens, splendor lucis aeternae et sol iustitiae: ueni et illumina sedentem in tenebris et umbra mortis", which means 'O Rising [Sun], splendour of eternal light and sun of justice: come and illumine the one sitting in darkness and in the shadow of death' (my translation).

Several antiphons are used as the basis for lyrics in *Crist* 1-439 (the section dealing with Advent). Every clause in the antiphon *O Jerusalem* is used in the corresponding lyric. Only the first three words of the antiphon *O mundi domina* are used in the corresponding lyric. The *O Oriens* antiphon consists of an invocation and a petition. The petition 'come and illumine' reappears in the lyric, but does the invocation? Does 'earendel' translate *oriens*? Does 'the true *leoma* of the sun' translate *sol iustitiae*? It looks more like the Blickling expression 'the *leoma* of the true sun', which translated *iubar ueri solis*. We cannot be sure. The trouble is that in OE the words for true (such as sooth, soothfast) also mean just and righteous. The just sun and the true sun could both be called soothfast, as in *Phoenix* 587, which Kennedy (1963: 246) translates "sun of righteousness". Only the addition of the word *leoma*, which seems to translate Latin *iubar*, makes 'true leoma of the sun' more like *iubar ueri solis* than like *sol iustitiae*. If an Anglo-Saxon wished to distinguish between true and just, perhaps he would use *rihtwis* for just; but I cannot find any example of *rihtwis* applied to the sun as a title of Christ. *Rihtwis* is the word from which we get righteous.

Cook (1909: 88-90) discusses *O Oriens* and *Crist* 104. He concludes that in *Crist earendel* means the rising sun and translates *oriens* and refers to Christ; in the Blickling homily "the new earendel is John the Baptist: the dawn or daystar preceding Jesus Christ who is the sun".

However, the superficial resemblance of this passage in *Crist* to the passage in the Blickling homily is striking. Tolkien did not think this resemblance misleading. He believed that in *Crist* as well as in the homily *earendel* was the morning star and meant the Baptist.

Earendel in the Blickling homily means *lucifer*, the morning star. Tolkien presumably considered the etymology of earendel, Aurvandill, Auriwandalo.[17] Ear- and Aur- could come from the root AUS which means 'bright'; from it are formed words for 'dawn', such as the Latin *aurora*. The second part of the word, (w)endel, vandill, wandalo, comes from VANDAL, a lengthened form of the root VAND, which can mean 'wander'; the Vandals were so called because they were wanderers.[18] In German, *Wandelstern* means 'planet, wandering star'. Tolkien perhaps decided that to the Anglo-Saxons *earendel* meant 'dawn planet, dawn star'; to the Norsemen the personal name Aurvandill may have meant 'Bright Wanderer'. In Tolkien's first poem about Earendel (*Lost Tales* II 267-9) he is the evening star; the first part of his name therefore is taken to mean 'bright', not 'dawn'. In *Lost Tales* (but not in *The Silmarillion*) Tolkien calls him a wanderer, and in both books calls him bright. However, Tolkien soon changed the name to Eärendil, which is the Elvish for 'sea-lover'.

Bede tells us (*Epist. Cath.* 128) that the sun can stand for Christ, lucifer for the Baptist, and the moon for the Church. Bede is writing in Latin, in which these nouns have the appropriate gender: sun and lucifer masculine, moon and church feminine. In Greek, as well as in Latin and all the romance languages, sun is masculine, moon feminine. In all the Germanic languages, including Old English, sun is feminine, moon masculine. Sun is feminine in Irish and Scottish Gaelic and medieval Welsh. All these languages belong to the Indo-European family. In those spoken in the warm dry countries bordering the Mediterranean, sun is masculine; in the cool rainy lands of the North West, sun is feminine. If climate is the cause, the first speakers of these languages may have felt that the scorching summer sun of the Mediterranean was like a fierce warrior; further north, where winters were

---

[17] See Förstemann, *Altdeutsches Namenbuch, Vol. 1, Personennamen* (Nordhausen, 1856), under AUS and VAND, VANDAL.

18 Brewer's Dictionary of Names says under VANDALS: "The notorious Germanic people [...] take their name from Old German WANDJAN 'to wander'".

long, dark, and very cold, the sun was comforting, like a mother.[19] Others would explain the gender of the word for sun by the psychological make-up of the nation or tribe using the language. The Germans had a different make-up from the Romans and French; see Iordan (1970: 87):

> Even the most insignificant linguistic developments are to be accounted for in the same manner, such for example as the gender of substantives in different languages – compare the words for 'sun' and 'moon' in Germanic and Romance.

We need not bring in psychology to account for conservatism. The French for moon comes from the Latin for moon, and therefore has the same gender. The German for moon comes from the ancient German word and therefore has the same gender. More strange is the fact that the Romance languages abandoned the neuter, and the Germanic languages kept it. Still more remarkable is it that English, unlike all the other major European languages, abandoned grammatical gender entirely: except in poetry, we refer to sun or moon as "it". Perhaps this was because the English are practical. Why should we, like the Germans, have to remember that knife is neuter, fork feminine, and spoon masculine?[20]

The Greeks and Romans believed in sun gods and moon goddesses. The pagan Anglo-Saxons presumably believed in sun goddesses and moon gods. Grimm (*Teutonic Mythology*, Vol. 2 p. 737) tells us that Norse poetry provided both Night and Day with cars (chariots, waggons):

---

[19] Ferdinand de Saussure would not agree. In his influential book *Course in General Linguistics*, published in an English translation in 1915, he argued that the linguistic sign (the word) was arbitrary and wholly unrelated to the referent (thing referred to). He would say that the German word for sun is feminine, but not because the German sun is milder than the Italian sun. Tolkien graduated in 1915; he must have heard of Saussure's views soon after the beginning of his academic career in 1919. He never accepted these views. Nor did Otto Jespersen, C. S. Lewis, Owen Barfield or Simeon Potter (cf. Smith, 2006).

20 See Potter (1984: 24-25).

> Night and Day are drawn by one horse each, the Sun has two [...] Probably the car of Day was supposed to run before that of the Sun [...] The alternation of sexes seems not insignificant, the masculine Day being accompanied by the feminine Sun, the feminine Night by the masculine Moon.

In Vol. 1 p. 225 Grimm says "We think of Balder as the god of light or day". Balder being male can be god of day (a masculine word) but not of sun (feminine). The sexes alternate sometimes in Latin and Greek: the feminine dawn is accompanied by the masculine dawn star, the feminine day by the masculine sun; the feminine night is introduced by the masculine evening star.

English poets, because of their Classical education, have often called the sun "Phoebus" and "he" and called the moon "Diana" and "she". I do not find this unnatural. Tolkien however decided that in his mythology the sun should be "she" as in OE and modern German; the moon should be "he". In *The Lord of the Rings*, Frodo sings a song at the Prancing Pony in which the sun "scarcely believed her shining eyes"; and at moon-set Faramir says to Sam "Fair Ithil, as he goes from Middle-earth, glances upon [...] Mindolluin". In *Silm* 99 the Valar chose the maiden Arien to guide the vessel of the Sun, "and he that steered the island of the Moon was Tilion". The sun was the last fruit of Laurelin, and this tree is called "she"; the moon was the last flower of Telperion, and this tree is called "he" (*Silm* 38). (Telperion produces flowers, not catkins. Its descendants, the tree of Númenor and the White Tree of Gondor, produce flowers and fruit.)

Tolkien took the idea of these two trees from the romance of Alexander. In the Greek original (Pseudo-Callisthenes, Ch. 13) the oracular moon-tree that Alexander consults is female because the Greek word for moon is feminine and the deity of the moon is a goddess; the oracular sun-tree is male. The oracular trees are not luminous; and their leaves are not silver or gold, except in the twelfth-century version later translated into English alliterative verse as *The Wars of Alexander*. Though the romance of

Alexander does not belong to the North West, this alliterative version does. It makes the moon-tree silver and the sun-tree gold, which reminds us of Yeats' 'Song of the Wandering Aengus' which ends with "the silver apples of the moon, the golden apples of the sun". Tolkien's Laurelin and Telperion are in the same tradition. Telperion sheds a dew of silver light; Laurelin's leaves are edged with gold (*Silm* 38). Telperion's last flower is silver, and Laurelin's last fruit is gold (p. 99). The Greeks and Romans would not have made this distinction, for they never called the moon silver or talked of silvery moonlight; they called the moon golden, as Virgil does in *Georgics* 1.431.

Aengus is Celtic; Yeats belongs to the Celtic revival. There is a Celtic element in Tolkien's mythology, but he did not wish his fantasy to be fantastic and irrational, like early Celtic myth. He desired the Classical restraint found in sunnier lands. He wanted to compose a large work in which every part should be subordinate to the whole, as in the *Aeneid*; there is no such unity in *The Mabinogion*. The Celtic mist prevents one from taking in at a glance the whole of a landscape or an epic; the clearer atmosphere of England permits it. That perhaps is what Tolkien meant (*Letters*, p. 144) when he said that the tone and quality which he desired was "somewhat cool and clear" and "redolent of our air".

RHONA BEARE was born in 1935, the daughter of William Beare, professor of Latin at Bristol University. She read Classics at Girton College, graduating in 1958. At Exeter she began a Ph.D. thesis, not submitted till 1974. From 1961 to 1965 she was Assistant Lecturer in the Classics Department at Westfield College, University of London. In 1966 she sailed to New South Wales to be a lecturer in Classics at Newcastle University. She left Australia in 2000 and settled in Bristol. In 1955 she read *The Lord of the Rings* three times. In 1958 she again read it three times, and then wrote three letters to Tolkien; his replies are in his published *Letters*. (At the bottom of p. 278 the correct reading is "an immense peak, snow-capped, crowned with or piercing a dazzling white cloud".) She has written a handbook on *The Silmarillion* and articles in *Mythlore*.

References

Baring-Gould, Sabine, 1967, *Curious Myths of the Middle Ages*, New York: University Books.

Beowulf, 1973, trans. by Michael Alexander, Harmondsworth: Penguin.

Bradley, S. A. J. (trans.), 1982, *Anglo-Saxon Poetry*, London: Dent.

Brewer's Dictionary of Names, 1992, ed. by Adrian Room, London: Weidenfeld & Nicolson.

Carpenter, Humphrey, (ed.), 1981, *The Letters of J.R.R. Tolkien*, London: George Allen & Unwin.

Clark, Kenneth, 1960, *The Nude*, Harmondsworth: Pelican.

——, 1961, *Landscape into Art*, Harmondsworth: Pelican.

Clemoes, Peter (ed.), 1997, *Ælfric's Catholic Homilies: the first series*, Early English Text Society, Supplementary Series, No. 17, Oxford: OUP.

Cook, Albert S., 1909, *The Christ of Cynewulf*, Boston: Ginn.

Dutton, Ralph and Lord Holden, 1946, *The Land of France*, London: Batsford.

Hammond, Wayne G. and Christina Scull, 1995, *J.R.R. Tolkien, Artist and Illustrator* London: HarperCollins.

Herzfeld, George (ed. and trans.), 1900, *Old English Martyrology*, Early English Text Society (London), Original Series, No. 116.

Hooper, Walter (ed.), 1979,: *The Letters of C. S. Lewis to Arthur Greeves (1914-1963)*, (originally titled *They Stand Together*), New York: Macmillan.

Iordan, Iorgu, 1970, *An Introduction to Romance Linguistics, Its Schools and Scholars*, translated, augmented and revised by John Orr, revised with a supplement by Rebecca Posner, (first published 1937), Oxford: Blackwell.

Kennedy, Charles W. (trans.), 1963, *Early English Christian Poetry*, New York: OUP.

Lampe, Geoffrey William Hugo (ed.), 1968, *A Patristic Greek Lexicon*, (published in 5 fascicles, 1961-68), Oxford: Clarendon Press.

Leach, Maria (ed.), 1949-50, *Funk and Wagnall's Dictionary of Folklore*, New York: Funk and Wagnall.

Lewis, Clive Staples, 2000, *Essay Collection and Other Short Pieces*, ed. Lesley Walmsley, London: HarperCollins.

Linklater, Eric, 1965, Foreword to Jacqueline Simpson, *The Northmen Talk*, London: Dent.

Morris, R. (ed. and trans.), 1880, *The Blickling Homilies of the Tenth Century*, Early English Text Society (London), Original Series, Nos. 58, 63 and 73, published 1874-80.

Pevsner, Nikolaus, 1956, *The Englishness of English Art*, London: Architectural Press.

Pheifer, Joseph D. (ed.), 1974, *Old English Glosses in the Épinal-Erfurt Glossary*, Oxford: Clarendon Press.

Potter, Simeon, 1984, *Our Language* (first published 1950), Harmondsworth: Penguin.

Smith, Ross, 'Fitting Sense to Sound: Linguistic Aesthetics and Phonosemantics in the Work of J. R. R. Tolkien', in *Tolkien Studies*, Vol. III, 2006 (1-20).

Squire, Charles, 1905, *The Mythology of the British Islands, An Introduction to Celtic Myth and Legend, Poetry and Romance*, London: Blackie.

Stevenson, Joseph (ed.), 1851, *The Latin Hymns of the Anglo-Saxon Church*, Surtees Society (Durham), No. 23.

Sweet, Henry (ed.), 1885, *The Oldest English Texts*, No. 83.

Tolkien, J. R. R., 1975, *Farmer Giles of Ham and the Adventures of Tom Bombadil*, London: George Allen & Unwin.

——, 1977, *The Silmarillion*, London: George Allen & Unwin.

——, 1983a, *The Monsters and the Critics and Other Essays*, London: George Allen & Unwin.

——, 1983b, *Farmer Giles of Ham*, London: George Allen & Unwin.

——, 1985, *Lays of Beleriand*, ed. Christopher Tolkien, London: George Allen & Unwin.

——, 1992, *Sauron Defeated*, ed. Christopher Tolkien, London: Harper Collins.

——, 2002, *Beowulf and the Critics*, ed. Michael D.C. Drout, Tempe, AZ: Arizona Medieval and Renaissance Texts and Studies.

Reflections on Thirty Years of Reading
The Silmarillion

MICHAEL D. C. DROUT

Abstract

In this personal essay I examine the ways that *The Silmarillion* works to shape grief and loss into order and beauty. Drawing on thirty years of reading Tolkien's work, but in particular focusing on the first time I read *The Silmarillion*, during the winter of 1978, when the great blizzard struck New England, I discuss how Tolkien's writing creates its aesthetic effects and examine the importance of nostalgia and the problem of Death in *The Silmarillion*.

The Silmarillion was first published in the United States in the Autumn of 1977. Waiting for me under the Christmas tree that year, a gift from Santa Claus mixed in amongst the various Star Wars toys my brother and I had coveted, was a copy of the book, the cover illustrated with a colorized version of Tolkien's drawing "The Mountain-path." I was nine years old, living with my parents and my five-year-old brother in Newtonville, Massachusetts, a suburb of Boston. I think that I first read *The Silmarillion* during the school vacation between Christmas and New Year's Day 1978, although I am not certain. I do know that I was reading *The Silmarillion* on February 6, 1978, when the great blizzard began in earnest. Since that time, my inner world has been shaped by Tolkien's great work. This essay is my effort to understand how this shaping has occurred and to explain the ways that *The Silmarillion* worked, as it still works, to shape grief and loss and fear into order and beauty.

For my family, 1978 was a very difficult year. We had moved to the Boston area from New York City in the bicentennial year of 1976 with very high hopes, but living Massachusetts was far more difficult than we had expected. My father was finishing his medical training as a Fellow in cardiology at the New England Medical Center and worked very, very long hours. Our relatives were all several hundred miles away and, although we had made new friends, we found it difficult to adapt to many New England mores. By the winter of 1977-78, my parents were in the process of separating and eventually divorcing, and it was clear to my brother and I that whatever roots we had put down in Massachusetts would soon be torn up as we relocated to New Jersey to be closer to the extended family.

On a much larger scale, things were bad in 1978. The U.S. economy was a shambles and my father's fellowship pay had not kept up with the extremely high inflation. Although we had expectations of better days in the future when my father's training was over, as it was he had to take a second job moonlighting at a distant hospital in order for us to afford to live on the first floor of a modest two-family house (the landlord and his family lived above us). The energy crisis meant that heating was very, very expensive. We had been used to living on the ninth floor of a high-rise building in New York City, where having *enough* heat was never a problem (too much heat was), so it was very difficult to adjust both to the new frugality brought on by the energy crisis and the typical New England approach to keeping houses chilly: I was always cold and my brother and I seemed always to be sick (he had to be hospitalized for asthma and pneumonia several times). To combat the constant chill, I developed the habit of sitting directly atop the radiator in the living room, my feet propped on the couch in front of me, a thin pillow keeping me from being burned when the heat came up. I rested the back of my head against the cold glass of the window and read *The Silmarillion* for hours as the thin winter light faded and snow dusted the branches and berries of the yews.

This is a long and self-indulgent preamble to analysis, but I think it is important in this case to establish, as much as one can, the psychological situation of this particular reader of *The Silmarillion*. As a nine-year-old, I was not 'alienated': I enjoyed school and playing violin and being on a baseball team. I was not 'depressed': although I missed some things about living in New York City, I also appreciated being able to play outdoors, to walk to a friend's house, to ride my bicycle. I was not even 'lonely': I had a number of close friends, both from school and in the neighborhood; my mother and brother were always home when I was and the family upstairs had become our friends. No, I was not alienated or depressed, those buzzwords of pre-adolescent psychology that obscure the specifics of an individual's life and situation. But I was *sad*, a much simpler word and a much, much older one. Here is Onions' etymology:

> A. †sated, weary OE; †steadfast, firm; †grave, serious; sorrowful xiv; deplorably disappointing or bad xvii. B. †solid, dense xiii (cf. *sad-iron*, sold flat-iron); dark-coloured (cf. G. *sattblau*, etc.) xvi; (of bread, etc.) that has not 'risen' xvii. OE. *sæd* = OS. *sad* (Du. *zat*), OHG. *sat* (G. *satt*), ON *saðr*, Goth. *saþs* :- CGerm **saðaz* :- IE. *setós*, pp. formation (see -ED^1 and cf. LOUD, OLD) on a base meaning SATISFY and repr. also by Gr. *áatos* (:- **nsetós*) insatiate, *háden* enough, L. *sat, satis* enough, *satur* sated (cf. SATURATE), OIr. *sathech* satiated, Lith *sotùs* satisfying. Hence **sadd**EN^5 sæ.dn (dial.) make solid xvi; make sorrowful xvii; repl. †*sad* vb. (xiv) and (dial.) *sade* (OE. *sadian*)
> (Onions 1966: 781).

As you can see, *sad* has very deep roots indeed, going back in similar forms to Indo-European and appearing in the Germanic, Italic, Celtic, and Balto-Slavic branches of the Indo-European language tree. *Sad* seems old fashioned and far less analytical than "alienated" (which can be traced back to the fourteenth century, but had a different meaning than is used today) or "depressed" (which, meaning downhearted, only goes back to 1621 and with clinical implications, only to 1905), but sad is more accurate. If sad things happen to them, people will be sad, and there is nothing abnormal about it and nothing to be done beyond waiting for the sadness to pass. Sadness is a part of being human. It is not something to be cured or treated. Knowing these things (and of course one does not really know them at nine years old) does not really make the feeling any less painful or life with sadness particularly less difficult, but it does perhaps provide some hope that sadness can pass, that it is an integral part of human life, that it is not to be feared.

My own sadness, which I remember very clearly and without rancor, came not only from specific events and situations (the impending divorce, the absence of grandparents and cousins) but from a much more general realization that, I suppose, comes to everyone at some time: that things had changed in my life and they would never be the same again. There had been beautiful, wonderful times in the past, but there was nothing that could be done to bring those times back. I think Tolkien was acutely aware of this feeling, and with far greater justification than I had at the age of nine. I was sad over the loss of the happiness that had come with an intact home and the fracturing of the assumptions of continuity, progress and stability that went with that loss. Tolkien had endured far, far worse, having lost, in order, his father, his mother, the Warwickshire countryside, two of his three best friends and his health.[1] But the fact that there exist other people whose sufferings are so much more significant than one's own does not really make sadness go away. However, my particular sadness as a nine-year-old, which was, as one would expect, inchoate and unclear, was forever changed by reading the work of Tolkien. For in *The Silmarillion*, Tolkien transmuted sadness into beauty, giving shape to grief, making loss and longing into art.

I want to be clear first how this did *not* work. I did not read *The Silmarillion* for consolation (as I did *The Lord of the Rings*, which has, since I was very, very young, always been an intensely important text for my father and me). The story of *The Silmarillion* does not change sadness into happiness. There is no Field of Cormallen, no sprouting of the *mallorn* in the Shire or return of Bill the Pony to cheer a reader. If one turns to *The Silmarillion* to find cheerful, optimistic scenes, amusing hobbit-talk, or an

---

[1] See Carpenter's biography and, more recently, John Garth's *Tolkien and the Great War* for a chronicle of Tolkien's personal losses.

encouraging moral message, one is headed for disappointment.² That is not the effect of the book, and is perhaps why readers who loved *The Lord of the Rings* were terribly disappointed by *The Silmarillion*. But a work of art can do more than comfort or encourage or distract or console.

For me in 1978, Tolkien's art was most manifest not in the beautiful passages of *The Silmarillion* (some of which are discussed below), but in the sweeping grandeur of the tragedies. I was not so much taken by the most important stories within *The Silmarillion* (Beren and Lúthien, Túrin), but by the epic sweep of darkness and the heroic resistance to it. In the winter of 1978, when the cold had formed a thick crust of ice on top of the mounded snow and the joy and surprise of the great storm had given way to exhaustion and cabin fever, it was easy to feel as if Morgoth was winning, as if the bitter cold we all felt was rushing out of the gates of Angband, as illustrated in this print I made that winter (see figure 1).³

I hasten to add that I did not believe in the literal reality of Morgoth or Angband or Beleriand. Rather, even at that early age, I recognized symbolic and literary reality: Tolkien had created a set of stories that worked—as have the stories of the Bible for generations—to shape my view of reality, to give me a set of symbols and motifs by which I might understand and, perhaps, shape and control it. Although Tolkien himself toyed with the conceit that Middle-earth was a real history of our world, perhaps located in pre-history,⁴ I did not feel that Arda needed that kind of historical reality; it had already

---

[2] This disappointment is perhaps one of the sources of the negative impression of *The Silmarillion* held by so many readers. For a discussion of other features that may contribute to this impression, see Shippey (2000: 261-63).

[3] I certainly do not offer this figure as great (or even competent) art, but rather as further illustration of the psychological "set" of the interpreter. The mis-spelling of Angband is perhaps illustrative of how deeply I had internalized *The Silmarillion* at that time: I never thought to look up the correct spelling of Morgoth's fortress, but rather retrieved it (incorrectly) from memory.

[4] See Kocher for probably the most detailed elaboration of this idea (1972: 3-16). Kocher's analysis is remarkable because it was written before the publication of the "Númeórean" materials in *The Lost Road* and Tolkien's working out of medieval histories in *The Book of Lost Tales, Part II*, both of which shed more light on Tolkien's attempt to link up his secondary world with the primary world.

Figure 1

achieved a higher sort of reality, true at a deeply imaginative level that was for me far more satisfying than a literal Middle-earth would have been.[5]

My favorite part of *The Silmarillion* that year was Chapter 20 "Of The Fifth Battle: Nirnaeth Arnoediad", nine pages of almost unmitigated disaster poured upon all the heroes of the previous chapters. Fingon the valiant, who had freed Maedhros and at least temporarily healed the feud within the house of Finwë was lost:

> But now in the western battle Fingon and Turgon were assailed by a tide of foes thrice greater than all the force that was left to them. Gothmog, Lord of Balrogs, high-

---

[5] This interpretation puts me squarely opposed to Tolkien's own interpretation of myth versus Gospel: the "myths" in the Gospel were not "lies breathed through silver," but were true (Carpenter 1977: 147). If the stories in the Bible were true (I personally cannot concede this point), then to me they are *less* beautiful than if they were invented.

captain of Angband, was come; and he drove a dark
wedge between the Elvenhosts, surrounding King
Fingon, and thrusting Turgon and Húrin aside towards
the Fen of Serech. Then he turned upon Fingon. That was
a grim meeting. At last Fingon stood alone with his guard
dead around him; and he fought with Gothmog, until
another Balrog came behind and cast a thong of fire
about him. Then Gothmog hewed him with his black axe,
and a white flame sprang up from the helm of Fingon as
it was cloven. Thus fell the High King of the Noldor; and
they beat him into the dust with their maces, and his
banner, blue and silver, they trod into the mire of his
blood
(Tolkien 1977: 193-94).

A dozen years later when I was first translating *Beowulf* and came upon "þæt wæs god cyning" (that was a good king) in line eleven I had a shock of recognition and a reprise of the feeling I had when first reading this passage: recognition of the style (the abrupt "that was…") and recapitulation of horror and sadness mixed with admiration for Fingon's bravery.[6] That feeling was even further developed a page later, with the last stand (much like the situation at the end of the Old English poem *The Battle of Maldon*) of the Men of Dor-lómin at the Pass of Sirion:

Last of all Húrin stood alone. Then he cast aside his
shield and wielded an axe two-handed; and it is sung that
the axe smoked in the black blood of the troll guard of
Gothmog until it withered, and each time that he slew
Húrin cried: 'Aurë entuluva! Day shall come again!'
Seventy times he uttered that cry; but they took him at
last alive, by the command of Morgoth, for the Orcs
grappled him with their hands, which clung to him still

---

[6] My recognition of another bit of Old English via previous exposure to Tolkien is responsible in part for my career as an Anglo Saxonist: I took John Miles Foley's Old English course at the University of Missouri (and subsequently changed my degree from fiction writing to medieval literature) because I recognized the phrase "wes thu hal" in the course catalogue.

> though he hewed off their arms; and ever their numbers were renewed, until as last he fell buried beneath them. Then Gothmog bound him and dragged him to Angband with mockery.
> (Tolkien 1977: 195).

It was this bravery and defiance of Angband and everything that could be mapped onto Angband that held me and made the fall of Fingon and the last stand of Húrin part of my personal mythology. You will notice that in this passage, even in the midst of some of the most violent and fast-moving action in *The Silmarillion*, Tolkien extends that narrative depth—which Gergely Nagy has called "the Great Chain of Reading"—noting that Húrin's valor, as described, must come from some source within a tradition of art: "it is sung." The imagined source is speaking through the narrator, and the memory of Húrin's deeds are understood as having been preserved for a very, very long time. This is part of the triumph of the hero: despite the defeat portrayed in the passage—and the other, very real defeats visited upon Húrin and his children in this most remorseless of Tolkien's stories—the very fact that "it is sung" means that Húrin's battlefield prophesy was true: "Aurë entuluva! Day shall come again!": It must have, or there would have been no song. The very existence of the song of sadness is reason for hope.

As our family life grew worse and worse in the winter of 1978, I retreated more and more frequently to a snow fort I had built in the back yard. The winds had whipped up an enormous pile of snow, twice as tall as a grown man, against the house and then scooped away a hollow inside it. By digging a tunnel through the high wall and then excavating the inside, I had built a snow fortress that no one, no matter how tall, could see inside. The only entrance was through the tunnel, which could be closed with a large block of snow and ice. Inside the fortress I had carved a throne, spraying the excavated snow with water that then froze, making it a chair of solid ice. Into the icy wall above and behind the throne I had carved out the word "Nargothrond" by jabbing the ice with an old screwdriver.

The symbolism of my naming my fortress after the hidden kingdom—a secret refuge invulnerable to assault, protected from the evils of the outside world—is perhaps obvious now, but then I thought of it only as a place to retreat from the yelling and chaos in the house. The irony was lost on me then, even if now it is all too clear.[7] Why Nargothrond rather than Gondolin, I cannot say (the latter kingdom is described as being more beautiful),[8] except perhaps that Finrod appealed to me far more than Turgon. Finrod was the Elf most interested in men and their mortality,[9] and he represented a kind of nobility for which I yearned (and still admire). Finrod held to his honor even when faced with the fore-knowledge of his own death and failure: "An oath I too shall swear, and must be free to fulfil it, and go into darkness. Nor shall anything of my realm endure that a son should inherit" (Tolkien 1977: 130). Finrod would never have allowed Húrin to linger, forlorn, unanswered, before the cliffs of the Echoriath (Tolkien 1977: 228). And his valor was the kind I could imagine for myself as a nine-year-old: not leading warriors to battle, but fighting alone and in the dark:

> But when the wolf came for Beren, Felagund put forth all his power, and burst his bonds; and he wrestled with the werewolf, and slew it with his own hands and teeth; yet he himself was wounded to the death. Then he spoke to Beren, saying 'I go now to my long rest in the timeless halls beyond the sea and the Mountains of Aman. It will be long ere I am seen among the Noldor again; and it may be that we shall not meet a second time in death or life, for the fates of our kindreds are apart. Farewell!' he

---

[7] Nargothrond was, of course, a fortress that was destroyed and which is the source of destruction for another kingdom: the Nauglamír, brought to Doriath by Húrin from the ruins of Nargothrond, leads to the death of Thingol and the destruction of his kingdom.

[8] And its description in *Unfinished Tales* has haunted my dreams for two decades.

[9] As confirmed by the eventual publication of the dialogue in *Morgoth's Ring*. But there must have been enough information about Finrod in the development of the character in *The Silmarillion* for a perceptive reader to recognize this interest in Felagund; I was not in the slightest surprised when I learned that Tolkien put his most important meditations upon mortality in the form of a dialogue that included Finrod, the *Athrabeth Finrod Ah Andreth*.

> died then in the dark in Tol-in-Gaurhoth, whose great tower he himself had built. Thus King Finrod Felagun, fairest and most beloved of the house of Finwë, redeemed his oath; but Beren mourned beside him in despair.
> (Tolkien 1977: 174).

On the night that I now look back at as one of the two or three worst of my life, when my parents had their most violent fight, I ran out of the house, crawled through the tunnel into the fort, pushed the concealing block of ice into place, and sat on the throne, by myself, in the dark. The moon came up, and the ice of my Nargothrond turned a pale blue. I remember watching the light shimmer as the wind whipped clouds across the moon. I was cold, but the wind could not reach me. Finally, hours later, I went back inside.

Of course the clouds blowing away and the moonlight falling on the ice were natural phenomena, but the effect was very similar to that of Tolkien's art: sorrow was transformed, in some way, into beauty. The pain and its source were not eliminated, but it was somehow more bearable. Even if the new things (the snow fortress, the stories in *The Silmarillion*) bring new pain, it is somehow different than what was there before; it has a shape and a logic that was missing before:

> They buried the body of Felagund upon the hill-top of his own isle, and it was clean again; and the green grave of Finrod Finarfin's son, fairest of all the princes of the Elves, remained inviolate, until the land was changed and broken, and foundered under destroying seas. But Finrod walks with Finarfin his father beneath the trees in Eldamar.
> (Tolkien 1977: 175-76).

Good things, beautiful things, are destroyed. But there is a kind of transcendent triumph even though the lost good cannot be rebuilt. The symbolism of a fortress made of ice, one that would eventually melt and become as nothing, is too obvious to require analysis. Its connection to Nargothrond may be somewhat tenuous, as Nargothrond, although it eventually disappeared, was the locus of various tragedies and the source of much destruction, but the general theme of a disaster followed by beauty appears throughout *The Silmarillion*. The beauty, whether it be of the green grass on Haudh-en-Nirnaeth (Tolkien 1977: 197) or the yellow flowers growing on the mound that covered Glorfindel's body (Tolkien 1977: 243), does not redress the harm that has come before. And yet...

I have spent at least fifteen years attempting to understand that "and yet...", and not only in the works of Tolkien. The object of much of my scholarly research, the Old English poem *Beowulf*, works similarly: there is not much hope in the poem, no real sense that after his death *Beowulf* has achieved an eternal triumph. The poet suggests that all that will remain is memory, as he has Beowulf say to Wiglaf:

> Hatað heaðomære   hlæw gewyrcean
> beorhtne æfter bæle   æt brimes nosan;
> se scel to gemyndum   minum leodum
> heah hlifian   on Hronesnæsse,
> þæt is sæliðend   syððan hatan
> Biowulfes biorh,   ða ðe brentingas
> ofter floda genipu   feorran drifað
> (lines 2802-2808)

> [Command the famed warriors to build a mound, bright after the pyre, at the edge of the sea; It must tower high on Hronesnæs as a memorial to my people, so that the seafarers, those who guide their ships far over the darkening of the flood, afterwards will call it Beowulf's barrow][10]

Sailors will note Beowulf's barrow as they pass and perhaps remember his story, but Beowulf himself does not seem to expect any eternal reward, and the poet suggests that the hero's death is also the death of his people,[11] those

---

[10] Quotations from *Beowulf* are taken from Klaeber; translations of Old English, unless otherwise noted, are my own.

[11] The dragon fight "...is the end of Beowulf, and with him dies the hope of his people" (Tolkien 2002: 143).

who would be expected to preserve his memory. There is not much hope in this depiction.

However, I am not sure that, although he interpreted *Beowulf* similarly, Tolkien himself felt this way about his own work. He was far more hopeful. When Huor has decided with Húrin and the Men of Dor-lómin to hold the Pass of Sirion to allow Turgon to escape back to Gondolin, he says "Yet if [Gondolin] stands but a little while, then out of your house shall come the hope of Elves and Men. This I say to you, lord, with the eyes of death: though we part here for ever, and I shall not look on your white walls again, from you and from me a new star shall arise" (Tolkien 1977: 194). That "new star" is hope: the hope brought by Eärendil marked by the literal star that appears in the sky, "Gil-Estel, the Star of High Hope" (Tolkien 1977: 250). It would make sense, and even be obvious, that the "new star" would be a consolation to me, a comfort in my nine-year-old sorrow. But it was not; I loved the beauty of the story, but I did not then believe (nor do I now) that a new star *will* arise from much suffering and defeat. And I do not think in fact that *The Silmarillion* works this way. The advent of Gil-Estel is the sign of a coming "eucatastrophe" (to use Tolkien's own terminology), but there are few of these in *The Silmarillion*.[12] Tolkien may have intended the War of Wrath to be one, but the chapter as it stands, perhaps because it happens mostly in very swift, skeletal narration, has a very different emotional effect than the horns of Rohan. Perhaps this eucatastrophe (the hosts of the Valar arriving from the West) is diminished in *The Silmarillion* because the price paid for it, the undercutting of the victory, is given more narrative space than the victory itself: the theft of the silmarils by Maedhros and Maglor and the eventual loss of the jewels makes much of the war seem

---

[12] Tolkien discusses "eucatastrophe" in "On Fairy-Stories" (Tolkien 1983b: 153). Minor eucatastrophic moments in *The Lord of the Rings* could be taken to include the arrival of Gildor and the Elves in the Woody End, the appearance of Tom Bombadil in the Old Forest and again on the Barrow Downs, Glorfindel's finding Frodo and company, the destruction of the Black Riders by the rush of waters, the return of Gandalf, the victory at the Hornburg, the meeting of Frodo with Faramir, Sam's discovery that Shelob has not killed Frodo. The major eucatastrophes would be the Horns of Rohan, the arrival of the Eagles and, overarching all else, the destruction of the Ring. For discussions of "eucatastrophe" see Rosebury (1993: 95) and Garbowski (1997: 25-31).

as if it was for naught. But for me this does not diminish the power and beauty of *The Silmarillion*; quite the opposite. Even though I knew that spring would come in 1978, I did not expect it to bring healing or reconciliation. It did not.

This last point is perhaps enough justification for the exceptionally personal nature of this essay: other critics could argue that the War of Wrath, the destruction of the peaks of Thangorodrim by the fall of Ancalagon the Black, the chaining and expulsion of Morgoth, the (temporary) recovery of the silmarils, and the reconciliation of the Noldor and the Valar, *are* the happy ending made all the more so by the sorrow and horror that has gone before. Certainly I could find my way to making an argument that the torment of Húrin and his children, the blinding and mutilation of Gwindor, the burning of Gondolin are important because they make the eventual triumph of the West that much more poignant.[13] But I would never really believe such an argument because my reading of *The Silmarillion* is so entangled with my own life at that time. Spring did not fix everything; Beleriand was ruined, the silmarils lost.

So the reader of this essay now understands my bias. And yet I can justify my reading of *The Silmarillion* despite the fact that it is overdetermined by my personal experiences. The theme of *The Silmarillion*, the great problem that Tolkien encountered in its writing, is the problem of death. Now this is not the most original insight; Tolkien himself said that *The Lord of the Rings* was about the problem of "Death, and Immortality" (Tolkien 1981: 284). But I want to reconfigure this problem slightly, because at least in *The Silmarillion*, wherein most of the characters are Elves, who do not die in the same sense as humans, it seems to me that it is not only death, not human death in isolation, that is at the heart of Tolkien's work. Rather, it is the problem of decay, of entropy.

---

[13] Tolkien in *Beowulf and the Critics*: "It has been said that there is mirth and music and gentle talk in *Beowulf*, but 'the light is but a foil to the dark.' This should perhaps have been reversed. The dark is a foil to the light. The dark is the background, and the light is encircled by it. But not of course because mirth and music were 'vain' and the light too fleeting for esteem. They were valued passionately" (2002: 115).

The Lord of the Rings may be consolation (certainly many readers have found it to be so), a meditation upon mercy and pity, an illustration, as Tolkien suggests, of the final two petitions of the Lord's Prayer, "and lead us not into temptation; but deliver us from evil" (Shippey 2003: 145).[14] But *The Silmarillion* (both Quenta Silmarillion and Akallabêth) are far more unforgiving, close engagements with death and entropic destruction, the theme (as Tolkien put it in "*Beowulf*: The Monsters and the Critics") "that men, each men and all men and all their works shall die" (Tolkien 1983b: 23). In *The Lord of the Rings* we lose Théoden, Hama, Halbarad, and many warriors, Boromir, Denethor, Gríma Wormtongue and Saruman, even Gandalf for a time. But of our heroes, the characters we come to know and care about, only Boromir and Theoden are killed, only Frodo so wounded that he must leave the Shire. Shippey notes that Tolkien was tempted to indulge in "kind-heartedness over minor matters" such as the evacuation of Minas Tirith or the survival of Bill the Pony, and that he struggled with scenes of pain (2003: 154-55, 319). But even 'hard-hearted' would be a litotes for describing the way Tolkien treats his characters in *The Silmarillion*: Miriel, Finwë, Fëanor, Aredhel, Eöl, Angrod, Aegnor, Fingolfin, Fingon, Beleg, Orodreth, Gwindor, Thingol, Celegorm, Curufin, Caranthir, Dior, Nimloth, Maeglin, Turgon, Glorfindel, Amrod, Amras, and Maedhros are all killed by violence or by wasting away, and those are merely the main *Elves* who die. Most of the more minor characters are killed as well—nearly every Man meets a violent death of one kind or another, as do all of the named Dwarves. In fact, at the end of *The Silmarillion* the entire house of Finwë has been decimated to the point that only Celebrimbor from the House of Fëanor, Elrond and Elros of the House of Fingolfin, and Galadriel of the House of Finarfin remain alive and in Middle-earth. Likewise the House of Elwë (Thingol) is reduced to Elrond and Elros. These two half-Elven brothers are also the sole descendants of the Houses of Bëor and Hador and the People of Haleth. The increase of entropy is evident in the destruction of every beautiful city (Menegroth, Nargothrond, Gondolin). The

---

[14] Shippey is quoting Tolkien from a letter to David I. Masson

silmarils are lost and Beleriand is in ruins. Tolkien is absolutely relentless. Death is the (nearly) inevitable end of his characters. This is partially the case because *The Silmarillion* covers such a vast span of time: in history; everyone eventually dies, and *The Silmarillion* is a kind of history. However, the deaths of Elves are *not* inevitable while the world lasts.

I think the deaths of so many characters repel many readers of *The Silmarillion*,[15] but it was exactly what attracted me to the book. Not because I was obsessed with death or desired it (quite the opposite), but because this was the first work of literature I had found that struggled with one of the most significant problems of human existence, and did so in a way that made sense to me. I have not made a systematic study, and I do not know how one would go about doing so, but my impression from my own experience and from talking to my children is that children certainly fear death (quite terribly) but do not *particularly* fear their own deaths. It is not individual immortality that is appealing to them, but immortality for others and for the things other have built.[16] And even at the age of nine we already know that such hopes are vain, that even something as seemingly solid as one's parents' marriage can be gone in no time, that even if that particular event had not happened, there were other ineluctable changes that could never be undone, the deaths of loved ones greatest among them: "But love not too well the work of thy hands and the devices of they heart" (Tolkien 1977: 125). No matter how strong and imposing the snow fortress is, it will melt and be gone in the spring.

Once we recognize the inevitability of death and loss, we are, I think, ripe for nostalgia, a feeling that has been (perhaps deliberately)

---

[15] I base this judgment on the reactions of my students, who universally love the Ainulindalë but are often alienated by the Quenta Silmarillion, and not only because the names of so many characters begin with "F".

[16] One of the most beautifully heartbreaking moments in my life occurred when my daughter told me that I did not have to worry about dying: "I used my birthday wish to make sure that you would never have to die," she said. Discussion with other parents of young children has convinced me that this particular wish is not unusual. Just before she died, my grandmother sent me a school assignment I had written in 1978 that she had saved. We students were asked to write down a set of wishes. Foremost among mine: "I wish that my grandmother could live forever."

misunderstood as a kind of tedious affectation, the indulgence of an old man endlessly talking about the great days of his youth. That stereotyping is a trivialization of a very central human emotion, and nostalgia is far more significant than its bad reputation would indicate. After all, if one has a happy childhood, or even a partially happy childhood, then nostalgia is a reasonable feeling *even if one's current life is also happ*y: that *particular* happiness of childhood is lost beyond recovery.

The word nostalgia itself comes from the Greek "nóstos" (return home) and "álgos" (pain): the Greeks recognized the feeling of loss that comes with the inexorable changes brought about by the passage of time: it is a pain not easily (if ever) assuaged. The real pain that is at the heart of nostalgia is perhaps most perfectly illustrated, with attention to the literal as well as the figurative meaning of the words, when Túrin returns to the pools of Ivrin and then to his former home:

> At last [...] he came with the first ice of winter to the pools of Ivrin, where before he had been healed. But they were now but a frozen mire, and he could drink there no more.
> Thus he came hardly by the passes of Dor-lómin, through bitter snows from the north, and found again the land of his childhood. Bare and bleak it was; and Morwen was gone. Her house stood empty, broken and cold; and no living thing drew nigh.
> (Tolkien 1977: 215).

The pain of loss that Túrin feels is repeated throughout all of Tolkien's works, even more so, perhaps, in *The Lord of the Rings* than in *The Silmarillion* (in *The Lord of the Rings* this pain is worked subtly throughout the entire narrative). The ache of nostalgia is perhaps even more evident in one of Tolkien's earliest works, "The Cottage of *Lost* Play" (my emphasis). A form of nostalgia is the curse of the Elves, who, in Middle-earth, use the power of the Three Rings to retard change, to prevent decay ("on the land of Lórien there was no stain" 365). But they, and their closest cultural kin among men, the Númenóreans, constantly run the risk of becoming embalmers, preserving the image of the past perfectly but unable to return to it. Nostalgia, for Tolkien and for others, generates a sad beauty, a love of both the past itself and the memory of that past. What is past is made particularly beautiful, colored by self-referential memory. In Tolkien's world this exaltation of the past—the nostalgia which can transform a grandmother's homely yard into a remembered Eden, a trip to the seashore into paradise—is again transformed. The Elves do not merely *remember* their past as perfect; it still exists, across the seas, in Valinor and Tol Eressëa, and the actual existence of this paradise makes their separation all the more poignant. These feelings of separation from what was once one's home, reflexes or further development of nostalgia, are in the end the emotions of an exile. Tolkien's Elves are exiles; Gildor Inglorion of the House of Finrod calls himself and his companions "exiles" in *The Fellowship of the Ring*; so, too, do the Noldor in Beleriand name themselves. An exile, too, is a young boy, shivering in the cold, coming near to frostbite within his snow fort when no one else in the house knows where he is or recognizes that he has gone.

War, famine, death of one's lord, the commission of crimes: these things all could lead to that condition most horrible to the Anglo-Saxons, exile. But there is another kind of exile as well, one that is forced upon *all* individuals, not just the guilty or the unlucky: that is the exile from one's past that is created by the forces of time. Time pushes relentlessly into the future, separating us further and further from childhood, then from youth, and all the time from those whom we have loved. One does nothing wrong to be forced into this sort of exile: it is part of the condition of being human.

In an unpublished discussion and partial translation of the Anglo-Saxon poem *The Wanderer*, Tolkien criticizes the traditional title of the poem, noting that "eardstapa," the word which has been translated as "wanderer," is more accurately taken as one who haunts the land alone.[17] The character in the poem knows he is not traveling aimlessly; he simply

---

[17] Oxford, Bodleian Library, Tolkien 30/1 f. 118; see Lee and Solopova (2005: 214).

cannot travel to where he wants to go, back to the warmth and joy of his past. The most moving lines in the poem occur when

> Þinceð him on mode þæt he his mondryhten
> clyppe ond cysse,   ond on cneo lecge
> honda ond heafod,   swa he hwilum ær
> in geardagum   giefstolas breac.
> Ðonne onwæcneð eft winleas guma,
> gesihð him biforan fealwe wegas,
> baþian brimfuglas, brædan feþra,
> hreosan hrim ond snaw, hagle gemenged
> (41-48)

[It seems to him in mind that he clasps and kisses his friend-lord, and on knee lays hand and head, as he at times previously had done, in earlier days, enjoyed the gift-throne. Then the friendless man awakens, sees before him the fallow waves, the sea birds bathing broad feathers, the tossing rime and snow mingled with hail].[18]

The power of those lines is not so much in the depiction of the warmth and companionship but in their loss, that they have been left behind and are only accessible in dream. The bathing of the birds and winter weather on the sea are both beautiful and stark, and they illustrate the pain of exile, the yearning. Likewise, for me *The Silmarillion* is so beautiful not because it is a consolation, but because it is instead a clear dramatization of grief, loneliness and ultimate failure. A few lines later in *The Wanderer* the poet writes "Sorg bið geniwad (50b) [sorrow is renewed]; the key word is the last, *renewed*: sorrow has come back; it is not new, it is part of a repetition of patterns of joy and sorrow that makes up our lives in this world.

We humans exist in a curiously doubled time. On the one hand, we experience time sequentially, and there is no returning. In Stephen Jay Gould's phrase, this is Time's Arrow. On the other, we feel ourselves to be part of many cycles, whether those be simple diurnal or seasonal rhythms or

---

[18] Quotations from the Wanderer are taken from Krapp and Dobbie. Translation is my own.

larger patterns of history: Time's Cycle.[19] Tolkien's works are intimately connected to the interplay of these two modes of temporal perception.[20] The inflexible passage of Time's Arrow can be terrifying in itself and is even more disturbing, perhaps, because it cannot be arrested. But Time's Cycle, while on the surface a comforting phenomenon, also has its dark side. Endless repetition leads to weariness with the world; the Elves at times envy Men the "Gift of Death," the freedom to leave "the circles of the world" and achieve some other fate. Time's Arrow also helps to avoid the repetitive stultification of Time's Cycle: "… in every age there come forth things that are new and have no foretelling, for they do not proceed from the past" (Tolkien 1977: 18), a statement that rejects historical determinism, a kind of which can arise from a cyclic view of time. And Time's Arrow and Time's Cycle blend into each other. Each individual life is unique, and yet the pattern of birth, growth and eventual death is the same. The death of a person is inevitable from the moment of birth—this is the tragedy, and the freedom, of being human.

Tom Shippey writes that Tolkien was continually pulled back and forth between two competing forces: "One was the urge to escape mortality by some way other than Christian consolation… the other was the total conviction that the urge was impossible, even forbidden" (2003: 327). I agree with the explication of this dynamic, but I do not think that for Tolkien the *langoth* (the longing) that Shippey describes is really about an escape from personal, individual death.[21] Even when Tolkien insists in "On Fairy-Stories" that "the oldest and deepest desire" is the "Great Escape from Death" (1983b: 153), it seems to me that he is really discussing the hope that *those things which one loves* will be spared death.[22] It is the fact of Death

---

[19] For a discussion see Drout (2006: 101-105); I take the terminology from Stephen Jay Gould's *Time's Arrow, Time's Cycle.*

[20] See Flieger 1997 for the most thorough discussion. See also Flieger 1983.

[21] Thus here I also (hesitantly) disagree with Ursula Le Guin, who, in *The Farthest Shore* speaks of "the traitor, the self; the self that cries *I want to live; let the world burn so long as I can live*" (1972: 135).

[22] Compare Letter #96, where Tolkien writes to his son Christopher that the "memory of this 'home' of yours in an idyllic hour (when often there is an illusion of the stay of time

rather than of individual death from which humans wish they could escape. And this wish is coupled with the knowledge that such escape is impossible. I know that I, as a nine-year-old would have gladly (and paradoxically) have given my own life to preserve my parents' marriage or the life of my brother when he was in the hospital or the world of my happy childhood.[23] But there was (in hindsight, thankfully) no opportunity for making such a sacrifice and no possibility that it would have had any effect had I made it. It is that sense of the *inevitable* loss that permeates *The Silmarillion*. One can go back over the narrative and play "what if?": What if Melkor had not felt himself slighted, or if Finwë had been content with his one mighty son, or if Fëanor had been willing to unlock the silmarils, or if Gwindor had not been present at Eithel Sirion to witness the mutilation of his brother, or if Túrin had taken advice only once in his lifetime, or if Turgon had led an exodus from Gondolin, or if Maedhros and Maglor had been willing to risk the mercy of the Valar...? But that is not the point of *The Silmarillion*. Had not these tragedies occurred, others would have, for that is the view of history and human nature that Tolkien held.

This uncompromising, pessimistic view fills *The Silmarillion*, and is due in part, I believe, to Tolkien's strong Christian faith: the world is the world, and it is a danger to the Christian soul to love it too ardently lest the spirit be tempted. I think there are few men who believed as thoroughly as Tolkien did that there *was* an eternal life to be had after death and so (to follow Shippey's line of reasoning) he was simultaneously very much in love with the world and conscious of the requirement that his faith imposed upon him to think of the next. This tension, plus the simple facts of Tolkien's biography, contributed both to a sense of nostalgia and a feeling that nostalgia was to be fought against, that it was in some deep sense a

---

and decay and a sense and gentle peace...[is] derived from Eden. Later in this same letter Tolkien discusses "the heart-wracking sense of the vanished past" (Tolkien 1981: 110).

[23] Compare T. H. White's *The Once and Future King*, where the youthful Arthur says: "If I were to be a knight ... I should pray to God to let me encounter all the evil in the world in my own person, so that if I conquered there would be none left, and it I were defeated, I would be the one to suffer for it." Merlin replies: "...you would be conquered, and you would suffer for it" (1958: 181).

rejection of the next world. But when you enter the world (note the focus on being *incarnated* in Tolkien's unfinished time-travel novel, *The Notion Club Papers*),[24] you are inevitably moving towards death. When you bring a child into the world you have set that child, whom you love more than you love yourself, not only on a path towards death, but on a path to being bereaved at your own death: you have created someone who will be heartbroken when you die. For Tolkien, the answer to these tragedies of being human was his religion, but for people who lack his gift of faith, there may be no consolation, merely acceptance: but that can almost be enough.

Throughout this essay I have discussed the bleakness and stark grandeur of *The Silmarillion* as it seemed to my nine-year-old self and as it ever afterwards has appeared to me. I have resisted the idea that *The Silmarillion* is a consolation, that the War of Wrath redeems the horrors, losses and destruction of the preceding narrative. But that does not mean that the experience of reading *The Silmarillion* was or is one of unrelieved gloom. In fact, my deepest notions of beauty were formed by sections of *The Silmarillion*:

> There they dwelt, and if they wished they could see the light of the Trees, and could tread the golden streets of Valmar and the crystal stairs of Tirion upon Túna, the green hill; but most of all they sailed in their swift ships upon the waters of the Bay of Elvenhome, or walked in the waves upon the shore with their hair gleaming in the light beyond the hill. Many jewels the Noldor gave them, opals and diamonds and pale crystals, which they strewed upon the shores and scattered in the pools; marvelous were the beaches of Elendë in those days. And many pearls they won for themselves from the sea, and their halls were of pearl, and of pearl were the mansions of Olwë at Alqualondë, the Haven of the Swans, lit with many lamps. For that was their city, and the haven of their ships; and those were made in the likeness of swans,

---

[24] See *The Notion Club Papers* (Tolkien 1992: 170-71).

> with beaks of gold and eyes of gold and jet. The gate of
> that harbour was an arch of living rock sea-carved; and it
> lay upon the confines of Eldamar, north of the Calacirya,
> where the light of the stars was bright and clear.
> (Tolkien 1977: 61).

If there is a heaven after this life, I hope it will look like Tolkien's Tol Eressëa. Tolkien's aesthetic, the balancing of the natural and the crafted, the living rock and the crystal stairs, the light and the sea and the gems washed by the waves—these are to me the heart of beauty. This beauty, however, is both in *The Silmarillion* and absent from it: the beaches of Elendë are in the uttermost west and only the Elves can travel there on the straight road. They are forbidden to Men and lost to the exiles:

> Si vanwa ná, Rómello vanwa Valimar!
> Namárië! Nai hiruvalyë Valimar.
> Nai elyë hiruva. Namárië!
>
> Now lost, lost to those from the East is Valimar!
> Farewell! Maybe thou shalt find Valimar. Maybe even
> thou shalt find it. Farewell!
> (*FR*, II, viii, 394).

The beauty is that of the ruin, the empty city, the fallen statue garlanded with flowers. On Aragorn's deathbed, Arwen says "there is now no ship that would bring me hence," to Valinor, to the West (*RK*, Appendix A, 343-44). We cannot return to our home that Time's Arrow has taken away from us, we can only experience the *langoth*, the longing for that home, the *nostalgia* that tugs at the heart, not in misery, but in true sadness that comes from the deep, inherited memory of beauty and one's separation from that beauty, what might be said to be the human condition itself, the recognition that one's life and loves and achievements are in the end ephemeral.[25] "In sorrow we must go, but not in despair," says Aragorn. "Behold! We are not bound

---

[25] Ursula Le Guin writes: "And only to us it is given to know that we must die. And that is a great gift, the gift of selfhood" (1972: 122).

for ever to the circles of the world, and beyond them is more than memory!" (*RK*, Appendix A, 343-44). The "more" in Aragorn's last words must be taken on faith.

The great achievement of *The Silmarillion* is to make this lost beauty seem completely natural, as much a part of the cultural history of the reader as the stories of the Bible were to previous generations. In that sense, and probably contrary to all of Tolkien's intentions, *The Silmarillion* entered into that part of my psyche in which the stories of Eden or Canaan or the wanderings of the Israelites must occupy in others'. This is not to say (at all!) that I have made a religion of *The Silmarillion*. Rather, Tolkien's work has provided a master narrative, the workings out of a pattern of building and loss, triumph and fall, beauty and wreckage that seems to me to lie beneath all of human history, both the immediately personal histories of individual lives and the vast sweep of peoples and nations. Tolkien created both the longing and the memory for which it longs. He made beauty all the more poignant for illustrating the unalterable truth that such beauty cannot endure for ever. Thus it is even more to be cherished, both while the time is, and afterwards, when it is cherished through longing. This vision has seemed to me, for thirty years, more true than any other.

MICHAEL D. C. DROUT was born in New Jersey in 1968, and is currently William and Elsie Prentice Associate Professor of English at Wheaton College, where he teaches Old and Middle English, Fantasy and Science Fiction, and writing. Drout is the author of *How Tradition Works: A Meme-Based Cultural Poetics of the Anglo-Saxon Tenth Century* (2006) and the editor of J.R.R. Tolkien's *Beowulf and the Critics*, which won the 2003 Mythopoeic Scholarship Award in Inklings Studies. Drout is the one of the founding editors of the journal Tolkien Studies and is the editor of the *J.R.R. Tolkien Encyclopedia: Scholarship and Critical Assessment* (2006). In 2005 he was awarded a Millicent C. Macintosh Fellowship. Drout has published widely on medieval literature, fantasy and science fiction, meme-based theories of culture and the works of J. R. R. Tolkien. He lives in Dedham, Massachusetts with his wife, son and daughter.

References

Carpenter, Humphrey, 1977, *Tolkien: A Biography*, Boston: Houghton Mifflin.

Drout, Michael D. C., 2006, *How Tradition Works: A Meme-Based Cultural Poetics of the Anglo-Saxon Tenth Century*, Tempe: Arizona Medieval and Renaissance Texts and Studies.

Flieger, Verlyn, 1983, *Splintered Light: Logos and Language in Tolkien's World*, Grand Rapids: Eerdmans.

—, 1997. *A Question of Time: J. R. R. Tolkien's Road to Faërie*, Kent: Kent State University Press.

Garbowski, Christopher, 1997, "Eucatastrophe and the 'Gift of Ilúvatar' in Middle-earth", in *Mallorn* 35, 1997, pp. 25-31.

Garth, John, 2003, *Tolkien and the Great War*, Boston: Houghton Mifflin.

Gould, Stephen Jay, 1987, *Time's Arrow, Time's Cycle*, Cambridge: Harvard University Press.

Lee, Stewart D. and Elizabeth Solopova, 2005, *The Keys of Middle-earth*, London: Palgrave Macmillan.

Le Guin, Ursula K., 1972, *The Farthest Shore,* New York: Atheneum.

Klaeber, Fr., 1950, *Beowulf and the Fight at Finnsburg* (third edition, first edition 1922), Lexington: D. C. Heath.

Krapp, George P., and E. V. K. Dobbie, eds., 1936, *The Exeter Book*, New York: Columbia University Press.

Nagy, Gergely, 2003, "The Great Chain of Reading", in Jane Chance, ed. *Tolkien the Medievalist*, New York: Routledge, pp. 238-58.

Onions, C. T., 1966, *The Oxford English Dictionary of Etymology*, Oxford, Oxford University Press.

Rosebury, Brian, 1992, *Tolkien: A Critical Assessment*, New York: St. Martin's Press.

Shippey, Tom, 2000, *J. R. R. Tolkien: Author of the Century*, Boston, Houghton Mifflin.

—, 2003, *The Road to Middle-earth*, (third edition, first edition 1982), Boston: Houghton Mifflin.

Tolkien, J. R. R., 1977, *The Silmarillion*, (edited by Christopher Tolkien), Boston: Houghton Mifflin.

—, 1980, *Unfinished Tales of Númenor and Middle-earth* (edited by Christopher Tolkien), Boston: Houghton Mifflin.

—, 1981, *The Letters of J. R. R. Tolkien* (edited by Humphrey Carpenter and Christopher Tolkien), Boston: Houghton Mifflin.

—, 1983a, *The Book of Lost Tales, Part I* (edited by Christopher Tolkien), Boston: Houghton Mifflin.

—, 1983b, *The Monsters and the Critics and Other Essays* (edited by Christopher Tolkien), London: HarperCollins.

—, 1984, *The Book of Lost Tales, Part II* (edited by Christopher Tolkien), Boston: Houghton Mifflin.

—, 1987, *The Lost Road* (edited by Christopher Tolkien), Boston: Houghton Mifflin.

—, *Sauron Defeated* (edited by Christopher Tolkien), Boston: Houghton Mifflin.

—, 1993, *Morgoth's Ring* (edited by Christopher Tolkien), Boston: Houghton Mifflin.

—,1987, *The Lost Road* (edited by Christopher Tolkien), Boston: Houghton Mifflin.

—, 2003, *Beowulf and the Critics* (ed. by Michael D. C. Drout), Tempe: Arizona Medieval and Renaissance Texts and Studies.

White, T. H., 1987, *The Once and Future King* (revised edition, first edition 1958), New York: G. P. Putnam.

Moving Mandos: The Dynamics of Subcreation in 'Of Beren and Lúthien'

ANNA SLACK

Abstract

This paper posits that Tolkien's theory of eucatastrophe, expressed tangibly in the workings of *The Lord of the Rings*, is also powerfully framed in *The Silmarillion*. In particular 'Of Beren and Lúthien' sustains a debate on the nature of subcreation and the way in which it can be integrated into the primary world of history through the performative acts of oath and song. The culmination of this is seen in Lúthien's song before Mandos, where the eucatastrophic 'second chance' given to the lovers in the primary, historical world is effected by a song reflecting the eternal. Although a short chapter in a longer work, 'Of Beren and Lúthien' charts a complex map detailing the ways that subcreation, here represented by oaths and songs, though always derived from the impulse of the same creative act, can diverge, bringing either eucatastrophe or dyscatastrophe in its wake. This paper also examines the effect of the loss of Lúthien, the tale's primary agent of eucatastrophe, and the way in which this loss ultimately affects the telling of tale itself.

> ...Though all the crannies of the world we filled... 'twas our right
> (used or misused). The right has not decayed.
> We make still by the law in which we're made...
> And stir the unseen with a throbbing string.

These lines from the poem *Mythopoeia* (Tolkien 2001:87-89) indicate the form of Tolkien's contribution to the critical debate on the interrelation between the eternal, primary, and secondary worlds. Tolkien argues that just as God made men, so men, fashioned in the likeness of God, make still because their fibre retains some consciousness of that initial creative act. Where Tolkien diverges from much of the critical thought preceding him is in asserting that the secondary world, the subcreation of man as represented in poetry, song and prose, can powerfully reflect the essence of the Creator. He argued that the land of faërie was uniquely suited to this eucatastrophic mimesis, presenting a stage whereon a glimpse of eternal joy could be performed without negating the very real possibilities of failure and sorrow.

The dynamics of subcreation, or the relations between and effects of performative utterances on and in the historical and eternal worlds, are set out at length by Tolkien in 'On Fairy Stories'[1], where these dynamics highlight the contrasting natures of eucatastrophe and dyscatastrophe. This paper posits that Tolkien's theory of eucatastrophe, expressed tangibly in the workings of *The Lord of the Rings*, is also powerfully framed in *The Silmarillion*. In particular 'Of Beren and Lúthien' sustains a debate on the nature of subcreation and the way in which it can be integrated into the primary world of history through the performative acts of oath and song. The culmination of this is seen in Lúthien's song before Mandos, where the eucatastrophic 'second chance' given to the lovers in the primary, historical world is effected by a song reflecting the eternal. Although a short chapter in a longer work, 'Of Beren and Lúthien' charts a complex map detailing the ways that subcreation, here represented by oaths and songs, though always derived from the impulse of the same creative act, can diverge, bringing either eucatastrophe or dyscatastrophe in its wake.

Striking Back to the Eternal: Tolkien's Faërie

In 'On Fairy Stories', Tolkien reclaims the theories of forms suggested by Plato and twisted almost beyond recognition in the consequent long train of critical debate. Tolkien agrees that there is an eternal, supra-human world, and that the primary or historical world exists below this and that it reflects aspects of that from which it is descended. But, contrary to Plato, Tolkien argues for the innate value of the secondary or created world of artistic endeavour as something that can go beyond the sphere of man and reconnect to the primal, eternal universe. In so doing he explicitly states that story

---

[1] Ibid, pp.1-83

continuously seeks to re-establish the severed link between man and the universe, the great dyscatastrophe of history. Tolkien's theory goes further, stating that the reversal of this severance is achieved in the life of Christ, for:

> ...this story has entered History and the primary world; the desire and aspiration of sub-creation has been raised to the fulfilment of Creation. The birth of Christ is the eucatastrophe of man's history. The Resurrection is the eucatastrophe of the story of the Incarnation.... For the art of it has the supremely convincing tone of Primary Art, that is, of Creation.[2]

In the Christian story, Tolkien argues, creation and subcreation go full-circle. The essence of the power of fairy-stories is that their scope is supremely suited to reflect the same process of despair being replaced by unsought joy, and in so doing to reconnect the reader to the eternal world. Eucatastrophe is when art enables us to grasp the joy of the eternal world.

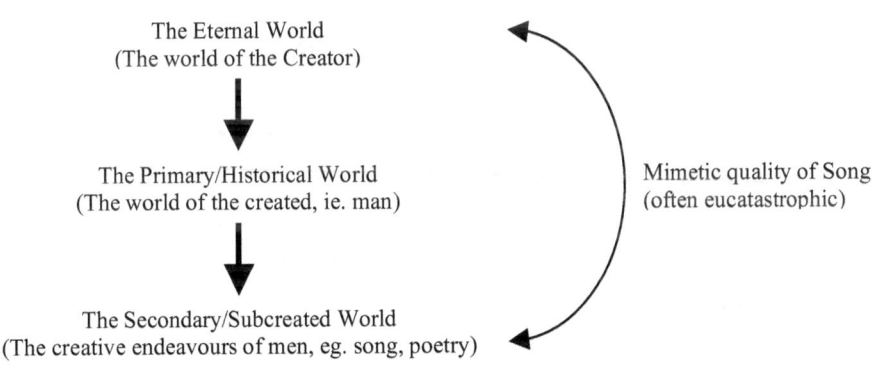

Fig. 1: Tolkien's Theory of Subcreation

THE BEOWULF SYNDROME AND THE EAGLE EFFECT

For scholars and critics, matters would be simplified if Tolkien's works always exemplified this subcreative vision where the text continuously

---

[2] Ibid, p. 72

points to the eternal. But as Tolkien himself noted in the preface to the second edition of *The Lord of the Rings*, he was not writing allegory. For the eucatastrophic to be a credible and effective device, especially in the post-World War era, there had also to be dyscatastrophe. Song needed a minor key to demonstrate the reality of sorrow and failure.

In *The Silmarillion* this is displayed in the influence of northern mythologies. In tone much of *The Silmarillion* has about it the notion of labouring under doom, and at times, as in the story of Túrin, this doom is inescapable. The curse lying over the Silmarils is the root of the long defeat that leads to the fading of the elves, and reminds the reader of heroes doomed to failure. This dyscatastrophic 'Beowulf Syndrome', as this paper terms it, is elegiac, and affords the scope to illustrate the tragic potential of man with heart-rending force. Its counterbalance is the 'Eagle Effect', the point where the eucatastrophic vision of the secondary world transcends the text and strikes back to the eternal, momentarily shattering the pervasive mood of its Beowulfian counterpart.

These two textual modes go together throughout Tolkien's works, rising and falling in an ebb and flow which is powerfully reminiscent of the primary world. They work powerfully in *The Silmarillion* as a whole, especially in the way that oaths and song are counterpoised in 'Of Beren and Lúthien' as both seek to affect the historical world of the text.

To understand a little more about the way these modes are used in 'Of Beren and Lúthien' we first need to consider the textual concept of the eternal world.

The Balance of the Eternal World

In the beginning was the Word, and the Word was with God, and the Word was God. He was with God in the beginning. Through him all things were made; without him nothing was made that has been made. In him was life, and that life was the light of men. The light shines in the darkness, but the darkness has not understood it. (John 1: 1-5, New International Version)

The beginning of John's Gospel is a useful departure point for considering the mythology of Middle-earth for several reasons. Firstly, like the book of Genesis and like Eru in the *Ainulindalë*, it attributes considerable power to the spoken word as a thing inherent in and innate to the creator and thus to the eternal. This dynamic gives supernatural value to words, and as such affects the transaction between writer and page, implying that the historical world can be altered by both the utterances and subcreative works of men, just as the creator's voice brought forth the eternal. But as in many mythologies this scriptural passage also introduces us to the idea that there is opposition in the eternal world, and that the creative moment is not comprehended by the 'dark' quarters who soon attempt to sow discord. The familiar terms of light and dark point to the two figures or groups of power that can be identified in almost any mythology; those that strive for the good, and those that strive for evil. Generally speaking, the forces of good aim to nurture and create, whilst those of evil try to destroy and unlawfully take command of what remains. The creative and destructive both accrue followers of their own, who follow the examples of their masters. In effect, we are left with two groups of 'creators', with one trying to wrest power away from the other.

In Tolkien's work, the *Ainulindalë* bears the burden of demonstrating the initial conflict between good and evil. It begins by presenting Eru as an unquestionable fact:

> There was Eru, the One, who in Arda is called Ilúvatar; and he made first the Ainur, the Holy Ones, that were the offspring of his thought, and they were with him before aught else was made.

Eru is placed in prime place at the beginning of this story, and all else is defined against him. This definition is wrought from the outset by identifying the narrator's passive position as a chronicler and setting this against the active verbs that demonstrate Eru's autonomy in creation. Eru makes simply by thinking, paralleling the *logos* of the Greek gospel of John, and his makings have a chronology that is recounted by the author of the *Ainulindalë* in such a way that Eru himself cannot be chronicled. Eru is a fact and truth whose own existence and history cannot be described; we hear directly of the making of the Ainur. This indicates that, much as in the Judaeo-Christian mythos, there is a rift between the created and the creator; the themes of Ilúvatar will be 'played aright' at an unspecified point in the future when all that Eru has created shall 'know the comprehension of each' (Tolkien 1999:4). By comprehension here the narrator indicates that the created will fully know as they are fully known (compare this with St. Paul's like statement in 1 Corinthians 13:12), and that at this time of full-knowledge discord and dyscatastrophe will be removed.

It comes as little surprise, then, to see that conflict arises through something reaching beyond its part: 'It came into the heart of Melkor to interweave matters of his own imagining that were not in *accord* with the theme of Ilúvatar' (Tolkien 1999:4, emphasis mine). Here the *Ainulindalë* is subject to an issue of reception amongst modern readers that it may share with *Paradise Lost*. Surely all Melkor is doing when weaving things of his own thought into the music of the Ainur is facilitating his right to create, a right given to him no less than to any other child of Ilúvatar. Why, then, does this expression lead to him becoming 'dark and terrible'? (Tolkien 1999:11)

Melkor's self-expression may seem noble, much as Satan's seems to many that study Milton's work. But Melkor's hubristic perseverance in his individuality embodies his arrogance, and is a stepping away from Ilúvatar's theme; he is an agent of discord when he ceases to be 'in accord' with the creator. In so doing Melkor becomes a dissident, creating out of his own mind at a time when it is only his place to be the channel of creative power. He misuses the subcreative responsibility entrusted to him, twisting the theme of Eru away from its intended purpose, and it results in his exile.

The friction between Melkor and the other Valar once on Middle-earth becomes a familiar battlefield between the good of the creator and the destruction of the dissident:

> And they built lands and Melkor destroyed them; valleys they delved and Melkor raised them up; mountains they carved and Melkor threw them down; seas they hollowed and Melkor spilled them; and naught might have peace or come to lasting growth, for as surely as the Valar began a labour so would Melkor undo it or corrupt it.
> (Tolkien 1999:12)

It is of note here that Tolkien, in his role as narrator of the *Ainulindalë*, chooses a rhythm of words and speech that imitates the half-line balances one might expect to encounter in Anglo-Saxon alliterative verse. For example, we might rearrange the text on the page in the following fashion:

> Valleys they delved   and Melkor raised them up;
> Mountains they carved   and Melkor threw them down;
> Seas they hollowed   and Melkor spilled them.

Looking at the text in this way demonstrates the ever-changing impetus that drives the work of the Valar. The destructive strength of Melkor's anti-creation is highlighted; the phrase 'and Melkor' stands like a wall in the centre of each line, seemingly hindering the verse that the narrator strives to create, and yet also becoming a stylistic feature of it. Melkor's own creative efforts, sundered from the creator, are in vain, but he can oppose the other Valar in what they create.

'OF BEREN AND LÚTHIEN': THE ARCHETYPAL TALE

The second part of this paper will examine the chapter 'Of Beren and Lúthien' as a remarkably concentrated illustration of the constant interaction of eucatastrophe and dyscatastrophe in a fictional mode which deliberately places them in closer proximity than might be expected in the realistic novel, together with frequent reminders of the power of subcreation, that is to say of the word, within the secondary world itself,

The interaction of eucatastrophe and dyscatastrophe and the differences between subcreation used and abused are highlighted at the beginning of 'Of Beren and Lúthien' in Gorlim's vision of his wife Eilinel. Here the false-creative strength of Melkor is show-cased at a human and primary level: 'There he saw Eilinel, and her face was worn with grief and hunger, and it seemed to him that he heard her voice lamenting that he had forsaken her' (Tolkien 1999:190). The narrator carefully stresses the insubstantial nature of the vision in using the verb 'seemed'. Gorlim, naturally enough, cries out; 'but even as he cried aloud the light was blown out in the wind; wolves howled, and on his shoulders he felt suddenly the heavy hands of Sauron's hunters. Thus Gorlim was ensnared…' (Tolkien 1999:190). The false Eilinel, a 'creation' of Melkor's, is nothing more than a phantom, portending death and betrayal. It is blown out by the wind. Contrasting this with Beren's first calling of Lúthien highlights the differences between the true and false creation. Beren's vision of Lúthien is acclaimed by the woods that join him in echoing her name. In these two incidents we see that, much as Frodo will later observe, the creative impulse of evil has the power only to mock the created rather than to make new. Another example of this grisly scope is seen when Beren's dream of carrion-birds sitting over the mere with bloodied beaks is transformed into a mocking reality (Tolkien 1999:191).

These events bring tragedy into the historical world, and are attributed directly to Melkor. They, along with the description of his efforts against the Valar in the *Ainulindalë*, frame Melkor/Morgoth as a spiteful being with the hubris of Satan and the overwhelming strength of Apollyon.

The conflict between good and evil is then enacted in the historical world, and moments of eucatastrophe reflect the creator while moments of dyscatastrophe seem to demonstrate the victory of evil at the expense of actors in the historical world. As Tolkien stated, the world of the fairy story is perhaps the only place where this battle can be figured properly, as the setting allows despair and joy better rein than some other genres.

SUBCREATIVE UTTERANCES: OATHTAKERS AND SONGMAKERS

In the Beren and Lúthien story we are presented with two specific forms of subcreation, oath-taking and song-making. Oaths are strongly tied to the weight of the world trammelled by Melkor, while songs are agents of eucatastrophe. By examining the roles played by each in 'of Beren and Lúthien' we are able to watch the tensions between eucatastrophe and dyscatastrophe, and to see how closely the two come together. It is this dualism in the text that ultimately demonstrates eucatastrophe so thoroughly.

We have said that the Middle-earth of Beren's time is one knit-round with mockery and destruction due to Morgoth's power. The driving force behind men in a world ruled by mockery is the binding power of the oath; where mockery pulls apart, an oath binds to a course of action or mode of behaviour. However, oaths are themselves subject to mockery, as Gorlim finds when Sauron promises him that his treachery will be repaid by the restoration of his wife to him. An oath is an indelible utterance that cannot be withdrawn; in response to the mocking birds and the fate that befell his father Beren swears an oath of vengeance, but in so doing must 'forsake' his father's grave. This word, itself of Germanic origin, implies the breaking of another oath; *for* is a negative prefix (as in forbid, fordone), and *sake* in its root comes from an old word meaning legal affairs and duties. The oath creates a future course of action that must be pursued, and, in this sense, we might say that it is the manifestation of the subcreative impulse in a burdened world. A man making an oath is seeking to create or call into the present a future state of being; in Beren's case, to wreak vengeance for the death of his kinsmen. This is a miniature version of the Valar singing Middle-earth into being, for there, also, words fashioned the course of the future. The difference lies in the fact that an oath can only be forged by navigating the web of words which bore it into the world, while song elicits new things. One is drawn, the other is born.

The power of the oath is in its ability to bind the speaker, and the great danger in taking oaths is in breaking them, or taking them lightly. Ironically, the restrictive power of oaths is powerfully demonstrated in Thingol's hall that, as a stronghold of the elves, is a place where we expect song to be at its most powerful. Melian and Lúthien, both associated with the web of the world and subcreation, are either silent or silenced by Thingol. The conflict between Thingol and Beren is emblematic of the tensions between oaths in the historical world; when separate oaths clash there can be no peace between them, as both parties have sworn themselves to a course of action. Thingol and Beren speak with oaths that mock the other, and this mockery ends by tightly tying them both to the fate of the Silmarils; as Melian perceives, Thingol's words have either 'doomed [his] daughter, or [him]self' (Tolkien 1999:197). The curse of the Silmarils is a historical agent of the Beowulf syndrome throughout the Silmarillion, and Thingol's entrapment in that curse (itself caused by conflicting oaths being made and broken) both literally and metaphorically lengthens the shadows in his kingdom.

The desire for and curse of the Silmarils comes to represent the danger of the subcreated thing misused in the primary world, but also highlights the abiding power in a such a thing. For the Silmarils also hark back to the eternal, and contain within them light from the trees of Valinor. It is of note that in the tale of Beren and Lúthien, the Silmarils are only agents of dyscatastrophe, being wrought about with oaths. The light of the Two Trees will only become an agent of eucatastrophe in the *Lord of the Rings*, when Galadriel gives the phial bearing 'the light of Earendil' as a gift to Frodo (Tolkien 1995:367). This demonstrates that it is not the created object itself which is good or evil, but the way in which it is treated by historical actors. In the Silmarils we are reminded again of Morgoth's egotistical pursuit of his own will against Eru's creation. In this way the Silmarils are forerunners of the Ring and link Beren's quest with Frodo's.

Thingol is not the only one whose words are distorted by the web of ill-will surrounding the Silmarils; in Nargothrond Celegorm's oaths to seize the Silmarils inflame rebellion against the rightful King. Finrod, however, refuses to be drawn further into the curse, choosing to keep his oath to aid Beren.

It is in Finrod and the other elves that choose to accompany Beren that we catch a glimpse of the power of an oath kept rightly. Despite his defeat by Sauron, the oaths of Finrod and his company in captivity hold fast in spite of the Werewolf which begins to devour them one by one: 'none betrayed their lord' (Tolkien 1999:201). None betray the identity of their mission. An oath broken or ill-kept brings mockery and despair, but an oath rightly sustained does not bring hope as we might expect; it brings only the inevitability of doom. Finrod's oath empowers him to 'burst his bonds' when the werewolf comes for Beren, and, typical of a world where glimpses of the eternal are slim, in killing the werewolf he earns his own death. In this act he fulfils his oath and saves his companion, but the redemption of his oath is not marked with any kind of joy or reconciliation:

> "[...] it may be that we shall not meet a second time in death or life, for the fates of our kindred are apart. Farewell!" He died then in the dark, in Tol-in-Gaurhoth, whose great tower he himself had built. Thus King Finrod Felagund, fairest and most beloved of the house of Finwe, redeemed his oath; but Beren mourned beside him in despair.
> (Tolkien 1999:204)

The redemption of an oath ends in mourning, just as it does when Beren finally delivers a Silmaril to Thingol. The death of Finrod looks forward to the redemption of Beren's oath to Thingol, and the parting of Beren and Lúthien in grief. The reader feels that in this Beowulfian world where song is suppressed and oaths cannot create any future other than one ending in death, the fate of two lovers caught in the curse of the Silmarils cannot hope to be a happy one.

Songmaking

In a text where the weight of oaths and Melkor's presence are so tangibly figured, the moments of joy represented in song are welcome. An example of this is Beren's first sight of Lúthien. After the darkness of his own journey through lands too terrible for description, this moment is a summer to both reader, narrator and to hero. As with Gorlim's fateful vision, it is evening, and Beren is 'enchanted' (Tolkien 1999:193). But the evening, a time of fading and deception, is counterbalanced by the 'unfading grass' (Tolkien 1999:193) and the immediate association of Lúthien with the eternal:

> Blue was her raiment as the unclouded heaven, but her eyes were grey as the starlit evening; her mantle was sewn with golden flowers, but her hair was dark as the shadows of twilight. As the light upon the leaves of trees, as the voice of the clear waters, as the stars over the mists of the world, such was her glory and her loveliness; and in her face was a shining light.
> (Tolkien 1999:193)

As well as being undeniably the most beautiful of Ilúvatar's children, the narrator here represents in the secondary world (the account we are reading) a historical figure who is undoubtedly an embodiment of the eternal. This tripartite presence from now on dominates the text, granting Lúthien heroic stature in deed and form, a stature often garnered through use of her voice, and her subcreative power. In this sense, she is a kind of eucatastrophe incarnate. When we first see her sing, the narrator shows us how literal the cycle of subcreation is; her song 'released the bonds of winter, and the frozen waters spoke, and flowers sprang from the cold earth where her feet had passed' (Tolkien 1999:193). Lúthien's voice calls forth things in the physical world, because her voice and presence are manifestations of the first voice that called forth the whole of creation. Beren is enchanted in part because he sees, even if he does not recognise, the eternal world in Lúthien.

It is this vision of the eternal that begins a subcreative process in Beren; 'In his heart he called her Tinuviel, that signifies Nightingale, daughter of twilight, in the grey elven tongue, for he knew no other name for her' (Tolkien 1999:193). In the absence of absolute knowledge, Beren creates a name for what he has seen, and on hearing her voice 'the spell of silence' (Tolkien 1999:193) falls from him. His own calling of Lúthien is echoed by the woods – the whole of nature calls her by the name Beren has given her, and Lúthien halts 'in wonder' (Tolkien 1999:193). It is as though the elven race do not expect to see such a subcreative strain in their mortal brethren, a strain that joins both the eternal and subcreated world. But it also joins them irrevocably to the historical, for it is here that doom falls upon Lúthien, and, struck by the name he gives her, she loves Beren. This complex conflict between the Beowulfian and Eucatastrophic is epitomised by the author when he describes Beren as 'slain by both bliss and grief' (Tolkien 1999:193); where his experience touches near the eternal in loving Lúthien, he reaches beyond a point of ordinary feeling. The sorrow is the dragging weight of the oath-laden historical world in which he is an actor, the bliss an echo of the eternal world for which he longed in creating a name for Lúthien. Lúthien, however, now becomes more deeply meshed into a Beowulfian mode where the oaths surrounding the Silmarils tie her to mortality.

In the power of her song, which will be demonstrated several times in the length of the tale, Lúthien represents the unadulterated strength of the Ea. This makes her a manifestation of Eru's power in Middle-Earth, and gives her an unprecedented skill in song as a subcreative art. The anguish of Beren and Lúthien indicates how in a world filled with false and mocking creation it is difficult to maintain joy. The narrator is always at great lengths to communicate to the reader the brevity of their joy, and in so doing heightens the effect of the Beowulf syndrome.

Apart from Lúthien the tale's other singer is Finrod, whose battle with Sauron in song demonstrates that the eucatastrophe of song is not always enough – especially when it must counter the doom of the Noldor, the oathbreakers. Finrod and Sauron are well matched, and Finrod brings 'the might of Elvenesse'(Tolkien 1999:201) in his song, figured in the memory of Valinor 'beyond the western world'(Tolkien 1999:201). But the memory of the kinslaying becomes a powerful movement in the song, and it is this that causes Finrod to fall:

> Then the gloom gathered; the darkness growing
> In Valinor, the red blood flowing
> Beside the Sea, where the Noldor slew
> The Foamriders, and stealing drew
> Their white ships with their white sails
> From lamplit havens. The wind wails,
> The wolf howls. The ravens flee.
> The ice mutters in the mouths of the Sea.
> The captives sad in Angband mourn.
> Thunder rumbles, the fires burn –
> And Finrod fell before the throne.
> (Tolkien 1999:201)

In this verse, Finrod's defeat at the hands of Sauron is figured as an inescapable consequence of the curse following the Noldor, who had broken oaths in killing their kin. It is the curse of this broken oath that trammels Finrod's ability to strive in songs more powerful than Sauron's.

Finrod's fall, and following death, are moments that are riven with the consequence of oaths, as we have seen, and the memory of each oath creates a gathering weight on the text that creates a powerful sense of despair, especially in Beren. But it is in this moment that Lúthien arrives, and the power of song is once again underlined:

> In that hour Lúthien came, and standing upon the bridge that led to Sauron's isle she sang a song that no walls of stone could hinder. Beren heard, and he thought that he dreamed; for the stars shone above him, and in the trees nightingales were singing...
> (Tolkien 1999:204)

Lúthien's song can loose and bind, turning Beren's prison into a starry world, and frees the captives following Sauron's defeat. But it also redeems the despair of Finrod's death, for his grave remains inviolate 'until the land was changed and broken, and foundered under destroying seas' (Tolkien 1999:206).

The apocalyptic vision portrayed by the narrator in miniature at Finrod's burial is a forerunner of the song that Beren creates on 'the threshold of the final peril' (Tolkien 1999:209) as he prepares to descend to Thangorodrim:

> Farewell sweet earth and northern sky,
> For ever blest, since here did lie
> And here with lissom limbs did run
> Beneath the Moon, beneath the Sun,
> Lúthien Tinúviel
> More fair than mortal tongue can tell.
> Though all to ruin fell the world
> And were dissolved and backward hurled
> Unmade into the old abyss,
> Yet were its making good, for this –
> The dusk, the dawn, the earth, the sea –
> That Lúthien for a time should be.
> (Tolkien 1999:209-10)

Beren for the first time accounts the world in which he lives good for the fact that Lúthien is in it. Her existence is set on a par with that of the moon, sun, earth and sea, showcasing her as a natural fruit of the creative hand that made them all. This fragment of Beren's song is defiant against the destructive will of Morgoth, and the restrictions of the world in which Beren strives, for Beren here bids farewell to the world and acknowledges simply the beauty and goodness figured in Lúthien. It is a selfless song, and maybe it is this aspect which draws Lúthien so swiftly to him.

The Contest of Oath and Song

We have seen that oath and song perform very different functions in the tale of Beren and Lúthien, but that these functions combine to give a realistic vision of a world trying to fend of dyscatastrophe and seeking hope. This combination of menacing failure and approaching good creates a faërie story in the way that Tolkien envisaged the best of such stories to be. This co-operative between dyscatastrophe and eucatastrophe is highlighted in the climax to the Beren and Lúthien story, where oath and song contest in confronting Morgoth in his hall, a place 'upheld by horror' (Tolkien 1999:212).

Lúthien's connection to the eternal through her song and her descent from 'divine race' (Tolkien 1999:212), bring her undaunted before Morgoth. It is her status as an heir of Eru and her beauty which kindle 'an evil lust' (Tolkien 1999:212) in Morgoth – a desire, the narrator implies, to thoroughly trammel what is in effect the last thing in Middle-Earth which still bears the grace of Eru's creation. The same song which throws all of Morgoth's court into slumber causes the Silmarils to blaze in answer with 'a radiance of white flame' (Tolkien 1999:213), making the crown in which they are set too heavy for Morgoth's head. It is the power of Lúthien's song that enables the fulfilment of Beren's vow as he cuts a Silmaril from the crown.

It is in this moment of eucatastrophic victory that the tragedy of the tale truly begins: 'It came then into Beren's mind that he would go beyond his vow' (Tolkien 1999:213). This moment of pride is to have results as severe as those that follow a vow unkept. The court begins to wake, Beren loses both hand and Silmaril to Carcharoth, and Lúthien's failing power is not enough to take them safely from the gates. At the final moment, the pride of an oath exceeded is enough to supersede the hitherto unassailable power of song that Lúthien bears.

Fortuitously, Beren and Lúthien are saved by Eagles who bear them back to Doriath. Though later in Tolkien's work the appearance of eagles will herald being saved from death (as it does for Bilbo in *The Hobbit*, and for all four hobbits in *The Lord of the Rings*), here their undeniably eucatastrophic presence cannot undo the certainty of death which begins to crowd Beren: 'suffering was graven in his face' (Tolkien 1999:215). Indeed, the quest of the Silmaril ends in despair, with Beren's death following the fulfilment of his oath to Thingol, and the falling of darkness on Lúthien. In this darkness she goes to the hall of Mandos, and from it comes her last song:

> The song of Lúthien before Mandos was the song most fair that ever in words was woven, and the song most sorrowful that ever the world shall hear. Unchanged, imperishable, it is sung still in Valinor beyond the hearing of the world, and listening the Valar are grieved. For Lúthien wove two themes of words, of the sorrow of the Eldar and the grief of Men, of the Two Kindreds that were made by Ilúvatar to dwell in Arda, the Kingdom of Earth amid the innumerable stars. And as she knelt before him her tears fell upon his feet like rain upon the stones; and Mandos was moved to pity, who never before was so moved, nor has been since.
> (Tolkien 1999:220)

In her final song, it is the grief that Lúthien has come to know in the dyscatastrophic historical world that enables her to move Mandos. Her song, based in grief, both does and does not work eucatastrophe. For Beren and Lúthien are offered the chance to return to the world, but are offered no guarantee of joy. Lúthien's last song speaks of the creation of men and elves in the eternal world, but is moved with knowledge of the historical world. In this way, Lúthien's voice unifies the eternal (in her recalling of the creation), historical (by means of her experience, garnered through life in the primary world) and secondary (shown in the song which she creates) worlds together in a more comprehensive way than before. In this respect, her song before Mandos is her greatest.

The Loss of Lúthien: Daeron and the Narrator

We have seen that the tale of Beren and Lúthien sustains a dialogue on the exact nature of oath and song as subcreative deeds in the historical world, and the impacts and forces behind each. It is implied that song, as a descendent of Eru's creative will, has the power to loose and bind due to the fact that it is creative will which draws back into the historical world memory of the original, unsullied creation. This will enables joy, though all too often the Eagle Effect is hampered in by the effects of oaths broken or exceeded. As the tale of Beren and Lúthien draws to a close there are touches in the text that indicate the narrator's own preoccupation with the loss of Lúthien, and the eucatastrophic ability that she represents.

The narrator of the Beren and Lúthien story is constantly looking to the unification of eternal, history and song, and employs the latter wherever he can, despite his assertion that his tale is without it. In fact, the prose moves in such a way that it very often suggests the eloquence of the song upon which it is based. But the conflict for the narrator is in being caught between the weight of the Beowulfian world in which he writes and the power of song showcased by Lúthien, now lost. It is this collision between the narrator's position and the story he is telling which imbue the tale with so much latent song and a kind of sorrow, even at the moment where Mandos is moved. It is as though the narrator of the Beren and Lúthien story found himself struggling not with the question 'quid Hinieldus cum Christo?',[3] but rather 'what has song to do with man?' It is the same question that Tolkien was answering when he wrote *Mythopoeia*.

This can be seen in the way the narrator deals with the fate of Daeron, the minstrel who loved Lúthien and later betrayed her love for Beren to Thingol:

> He it was that made music for the dance and song of
> Lúthien, before Beren came to Doriath; and he had loved

---

[3] 'What has Ingeld to do with Christ?', Alcuin in a letter to the Bishop of Lindisfarne, AD 797

> her, and set all his thought of her in his music. He became the greatest of all the minstrels of the Elves east of the Sea, named even before Maglor son of Feanor. But seeking for Lúthien in despair he wandered upon strange paths, and passing over the mountains he came into the East of Middle-earth, where for many ages he made lament beside dark waters for Lúthien, daughter of Thingol, most beautiful of all living things.
> (Tolkien 1999:216)

At first glance we might put this tale in the same category as Gorlim's dream, a tragic moment representing the weight of the Beowulf syndrome on the text and foreboding the sense of grief that will befall at Lúthien's death. But in this picture of Daeron there are echoes of the narrator of the tale, for it reflects the elegiac note that dominates the text. It is as though the narrator himself laments the loss of Lúthien, and it is this loss which has so powerfully moved his tale. In recounting Lúthien's story the narrator laments her passing from the world, but he has in that lament sought to reach the eternal world which she typified. That nobody 'saw Beren or Lúthien leave the world, nor marked where their bodies lay' (Tolkien 1999:222) is in many ways a fitting conclusion for the narrative. This ending elevates both Beren and Lúthien to a realm of myth that is in step with the impetus of the eternal world, but which has no reconciliation for their going. The loss of Lúthien is felt by the narrator of *The Silmarillion* throughout the rest of his chronicles, and, more generally, is felt throughout Tolkien's work as the elves as a whole begin to fade.

It is in this way that the grief of *The Silmarillion*'s narrator reflects Tolkien himself. By association with Lúthien the elves become representative in the *Lord of the Rings* of the eucatastrophic and eternal forces that move the world, and their withdrawal to Valinor, much as Lúthien's death, is an elegy for a sense of the eternal missing from our own historical world. Tolkien, a 'singer' bringing forth a whole world in his work, feels the weight of our own world in his writing, and the sorrow at

Lúthien's loss is perhaps a reflection of Tolkien's sorrow at the pervading mood of his time[4].

LÚTHIEN'S LEGACY: THE 'THROBBING STRING'

Lúthien's loss does not end the connection between song and the eternal: the power of song to denounce and overpower the work of evil and enable life and hope in its stead will be edified again in Sam's song at Cirith Ungol. Here the memory of the story of Beren and Lúthien, figured linguistically in the 'elven stars' (Tolkien 1995:888) and Sam's assertion that he, unlike Beren in his song of Parting, will not 'bid the stars farewell' (Tolkien 1995:888), unbinds despair in Sam's historical world when his song is answered. This is one example of many in Tolkien's works, but its scope is to show that eucatastrophe is not tied exclusively to Lúthien, though she represents it strongly. She is a reminder of the ability of song to strike through the dyscatastrophe of the historical world, and her last song is a powerful statement of both the value of dyscatastrophe and the power of eucatastrophe. It is the stirring of the unseen 'with a throbbing string' (Tolkien 2001:89), prefigured so powerfully in her song before Mandos, that is Lúthien's legacy to Middle-Earth.

ANNA SLACK is a teacher of English Language at a private language school in Palermo, Sicily. She graduated with a first class degree in English Literature from the University of Cambridge in 2005, and hopes to undertake research later. She spent two years editing the journal of the Cambridge Tolkien Society, *Anor*, and a year as the society secretary. She helped pioneer and took part in an acclaimed performance of the BBC Radio Adaptation of *The Lord of the Rings* in aid of the National Trust. Anna delivered a lecture at the Tolkien 2005 conference in Birmingham which was published last year in the Walking Tree volume *Tolkien and Modernity*.

---

[4] For further discussion, see Slack (2006: 115ff).

References

Slack, Anna, 2006, 'Slow-Kindled Courage: A Study of Heroes in the Works of J.R.R. Tolkien', in *Tolkien and Modernity* Vol. II, ed. Frank Weinreich and Thomas Honegger, Zurich and Berne: Walking Tree Publishers, pp. 115-141.

The Concise Oxford English Dictionary, ed. Catherine Soanes and Angus Stevenson, (eleventh edition, first edition 1911), Oxford: Oxford University Press.

The Holy Bible New International Version, (first edition 1973), London: Hodder & Stoughton.

Tolkien, J.R.R., 1995, *The Lord of the Rings*, (fourth edition, first one-volume edition 1968), London: HarperCollins.

——, 1999, *The Silmarillion*, edited by Christopher Tolkien (third edition, first edition 1977), London: HarperCollins.

——, 2001, *Tree and Leaf*, (fourth edition, first edition 1964), London: HarperCollins.

The Origins of the *Ainulindalë*: The Present State of Research

MICHAËL DEVAUX

To Father Jean-Robert Armogathe[1]

Abstract

This article sets out to present the current state of research on the *Ainulindalë*, identifying tendencies in its interpretation with reference to all the articles published on this topic since 1977. However, since some analyses of particular points depend for their authority only on the evidence of the final version, it has been necessary to trace the evolution of the text. By comparing all the versions published in *The History of Middle-earth*, it is possible to determine those elements which were present from the first version onwards, those which are found in one version only, and finally the changes which radically affect the whole conception of the cosmos, chiefly in version C*. Particular emphasis is placed on the second music and the figure of Melkor to show the developments in Tolkien's thought and the place of Catholic elements in his conception.

As every science fiction fan knows, *A beginning is a very delicate time*. I shall consider here the question of origins in the work of the person who is considered the master of high fantasy: is the account of the creation which lies at the heart of the subcreation of the world of Arda compatible, if not with that of Genesis, then at least with the faith of a Catholic like Tolkien? If so, why? And since when? For although a theologisation of the legendarium can be observed from 1937 onwards,[2] it is equally clear that at the beginning

---

[1] The idea for this article emerged from a Tolkien seminar held at the Almonry of the École Normale Supérieure in the Rue d'Ulm in 1995-6. Therefore it seemed appropriate to dedicate it to the Almoner.

[2] See Agøy (1998: 16f.); Apeland (1998: 46f.) (situating the major break in 1937); and Burns (1998: 9).

of the composition of *The Book of Lost Tales* Tolkien was thinking more in terms of a mythological tale, and perhaps also of the Scandinavian world. In addition it can also be seen that the *Ainulindalë* as it appears in the *Silmarillion* takes in a large part of the first drafts of 1918. This raises the question of whether there was a theologisation in the case of the *Ainulindalë* too. How far is it possible to distinguish the elements of Christianity and those of the Northern matter for any given period?

To answer these questions, firstly we have a well-established and signposted corpus: from the 'Music of the Ainur' in the *Book of Lost Tales* to the latest versions of the *Ainulindalë*, Christopher Tolkien has published a very large part of his father's texts in *History of Middle-Earth* (HoME) I, V and X. Secondly, the twenty or so critical studies devoted to the *Ainulindalë* have concentrated up to now essentially on the text of the *Silmarillion*.[3] However, it is characteristic that they do not appear in bibliographies; apart from very rare exceptions, the other articles devoted to the *Ainulindalë* are unknown. As a part of my investigation I shall attempt to draw some conclusions from the whole range of these studies, which I hope will bring some new, integrated and therefore practical insights. Thirdly, I have already presented a method to obtain a reading of the texts from *The History of Middle-earth*, in which I suggested distinguishing for each of the versions of a tale those features which are original, those which are subsequent, those which are unique, and those which are fundamental.[4] There, I used examples taken from the *Ainulindalë* for the purpose of presenting this method. Here I propose to develop and test it. This will make it possible to appreciate more

---

[3] Only the articles by John William Houghton, Fabricio Ciceri and Fabienne Claire Caland take into account the version from *The Book of Lost Tales*; Fr. Ricardo Irigaray (1999: 27, 42) also quotes the complete title of the last version, and gives a complete chronology of the different versions. It was only in the final stages of writing this article that I discovered the article 'Ainulindalen' by Thomas Giessl in *Hither Shore*, then in press, which deals principally with the role of Melkor in the different versions. I am grateful to Thomas Fornet-Ponse for allowing me to read this article before its publication.

[4] See Devaux (2004). (English summary by Shaun F. D. Hugues, in *The Tolkien Review*, 3, 2006, p. 202). *Translator's note:* The original French terms for these categories are *originel*, *originaire*, *original* and *fondamental*. These variations on a theme, difficult to capture in translation, echo and explain the title of this article, which also plays upon the Catholic origins and influences.

clearly how successful the *Silmarillion* is, but also to see the layers of which it is made up.[5]

I. PRELIMINARIES

Before embarking on the actual study of the texts, three short preliminaries are necessary. First, to recall the history of the composition of the different versions of the *Ainulindalë*; then to explain what is meant by the categories of original, subsequent, unique and fundamental; and finally to outline the plan of the creation according to the *Ainulindalë*.

A. Versions and dates[6]

Following Christopher Tolkien, we can distinguish between several versions of the *Ainulindalë*. The history of its rewriting is unusual and unique in that there is a direct tradition from one manuscript to the next (HoME I, 61).[7]

1) The first version (A), which constitutes the second tale in the *Book of Lost Tales* dates from between November 1918 and spring 1920.[8] The text exists in the form of two manuscripts: the version designated (here) as A-A is written in pencil on loose sheets (without a title), and version A-B is written in ink in an exercise book. This latter version is titled 'Music of the Ainur', and it is published in full in HoME I, 52-60. From an internal point of view, the narrator is Rúmil instructing Eriol.

---

[5] This short article is to be considered as work in progress, or at least a presentation of the state of international research on the *Ainulindalë*, including my own, without going into all the depth that would be possible.

[6] The following is a condensation of Christopher Tolkien's presentations in HoME I, 45, 52, 61-63; V, 155-156; and X, 3-8, 29-30, 39-40. Cf. the parallel listing by Thomas Giessl (2006: 152-157).

[7] Christopher Tolkien writes of "extremely puzzling facts in the history of the rewriting of the *Ainulindalë*" (HoME X, 3). Cf. HoME X, 7 : "The remodelling that constituted C out of B was in fact done at different times, and is in places chaotic, full of changes and substitutions".

[8] See HoME I, 45, referring to the letter to Christopher Bretherton of 16th July 1964 (*Letters*, p. 345).

2) The second version (B) dates from the late 1930s.⁹ This version exists in the form of two manuscripts. Version B-A clearly derives directly from version A,¹⁰ initially without a title, though Tolkien later added 'The Music of the Ainur'. Version B-B copies version B-A very closely, modifying a number of minor points, and is titled 'Ainulindalë / The music of the Ainur (...)'. This latter version (B-B) is published in full in *The Lost Road* (HoME V, 156-164). From an internal point of view, it is the work of Rúmil.

3) The three other versions are published in *Morgoth's Ring* (HoME X). Version C (later than version C*) is found physically in the same manuscript as version B-B, over-writing it, correcting it and using the versos. This version dates from 1948 and is published *in extenso* (HoME X, 8-22). From an internal point of view, according to the teaching that Ælfwine received from Pengoloð it is a text composed by Rúmil (HoME X, 8).

4) Version C* is a typescript which shows changes in comparison with B-B/C, and which must have been preceded by a manuscript (dating from 1946 according to HoME X, 6), of which only one sheet remains. (The relationship between B-B/C and C* will be dealt with below.) This version is not published *in extenso* (HoME X, 39-44).

5) The *terminus ad quem* for version D is 1948-1951.¹¹ Version D-A is a manuscript with illuminations and Old English abbreviations. The text has been emended in places. *Ainulindalë* is written in tengwar. This version (D-A) is not published *in extenso* (HoME X, 30-37). A typescript (D-B) represents a fair copy of D-A, incorporating some minor changes; only the notes on the first page merit attention (HoME X, 39). From an internal point of view, version D is a text composed by Rúmil, written down according to the teaching which Ælfwine received from Pengoloð (HoME X, 30).

---

[9] Before the end of 1937, see HoME V, 200, 207 (§1) and 165, n. 20.

[10] See HoME V, 155. B-A contains numerous emendations which represent immediate corrections made during the copying of A.

[11] See the linguistic arguments in favour of 1951 in HoME X, 7. However, Christopher Tolkien believes that D follows very soon after C, which would make it 1948.

The principal elements may be summed up in the form of a chronological table.[12]

Version A	Version B	Version C*	Version C	Version D
1918-1920	Before 1938	1946-1948	1948	1948-1951
Ms A-A	Ms B-A	Loose sheet		**Ms D-A**
Ms A-B	Ms B-B	Ts C*	Ms (B-B/)C	HoME X,
HoME I,	HoME V,	HoME X,	HoME X,	30-37
52-60	156-164	39-44	8-22	Ts D-B, p. 39

B. Original, subsequent, unique and fundamental

By *original* is meant those features which belong to the myth from its inception. This distinction may be refined by considering different degrees of originality. *Original* in the strict sense is used to designate only what is present from the first version on. Anything which is introduced at a later stage and remains to the end (i.e. from version *n* on) will be called *subsequent*. *Unique* designates features which are found only in one version or a group of versions; and finally *fundamental* is used for anything which conveys an overall concept.

C. The plan of the creation according to the Ainulindalë

Tolkien summarised the *Ainulindalë* at least three times: in his letters (1951 and 1964), and in his Notes to the Commentary on the *Athrabeth* (1959), all after the final version of the *Ainulindalë* had been produced. In the letter to Milton Waldman from late 1951,[13] Tolkien insists on the pre-existence (and therefore the initial exteriority) of the Ainur in relation to the creation of the world, and on their having known the world at first as a drama or story which is then made real. Therefore three periods can be distinguished: the time of the Ainur (before the world), the world perceived as a story or

---

[12] Key: Ms = manuscript; Ts = typescript; double underlining indicates that the text is printed in full; single underlining denotes that only the variants are printed; the versions that are not underlined are not printed or are referred to only in notes.

[13] See HoME X, 3 for the dating.

drama, and the history of the created world. In the letter to Christopher Bretherton of 16th July 1964, Tolkien emphasizes three other aspects: the Ainur are the first created beings, they have played a role in the realisation of the first Design, and the creator has introduced something new into this design (the coming of elves and men).

Tolkien was to state subsequently that the creation according to the *Ainulindalë* comprises five stages: "According to the *Ainulindalë* there were five stages in Creation. a. The creation of the Ainur. b. The communication by Eru of his Design to the Ainur. c. The Great Music, which was as it were a rehearsal, and remained in the stage of thought or imagination. d. The 'Vision' of Eru, which was again only a foreshowing of possibility, and was incomplete. e. The Achievement, which is still going on" (HoME X, 336).

If we tabulate this information (bearing in mind of course the contents of the *Ainulindalë* of 1977), we get the following schema.

1951	1959	1964
Pre-existence of the Ainur in the world	Creation of the Ainur	God creates the Ainur first of all
	Communication of the Design	
The Ainur perceive the world as a history or drama	The Great Music	Eru introduces the theme of the Children of God into the Design
	The Vision	
History of the created world	The Realisation which is carried out	The Ainur participate in the realisation of the Design

The most logical and progressive text is that of 1959, which distinguishes in relation to the world: the Design, the Music, the Vision, the Realisation. Commentators, when they have not restricted themselves simply to a summary of the text,[14] have proposed a plan in three (or four) parts; which is undoubtedly the *narrative* plan, which can be most easily remembered.[15] In particular Whittingham (1998: 212, 216f.) distinguishes between the Design,

---

[14] See also Houghton (2002: 177f.) and Cough (1999: 4f.).
[15] Tolkien's first two logical stages amount only to an outline, while the other three divide the text into major sections of noticeably equal length.

the Music and the Vision.[16] If these are the lines of force of the *Ainulindalë*, let us now pause to see if they are original. In this article, which is necessarily limited, I shall concentrate on the five stages identified by Tolkien. Although that will rule out some lines of investigation, it will make it possible to focus on the structure of the text and to appreciate the changes in the lines of force from the point of view of my main topic, the relationship of the accounts of the creation to Tolkien's Catholic faith and to his sub-creation.

II. ORIGINS AND FUNDAMENTALS

While in the *Book of Lost Tales* the 'Music of the Ainur' is only the second tale (after 'The Cottage of Lost Play'), from version B on it appears as an independent work, distinct from the *(Quenta) Silmarillion* proper (HoME V, 155). The *Valaquenta* in its turn was to become independent only at a late stage, in 1958 (see HoME X, 200).

A. Original

1) The Vision

The Design is already present in version A: "Upon a time Ilúvatar propounded a mighty design of his heart to the Ainur" (HoME I, 53). This design becomes a theme from version B: "And it came to pass that Ilúvatar called together all the Ainur, and declared to them a mighty theme" (HoME V, 156; X, 8).

Eru's desire for a Great music of the Ainur is also present from version A-A: "It is my desire now that ye make a great and glorious music and a singing of this theme" (HoME I, 53).[17] So are the Ainur who carry it

---

[16] Caldecott (2003: 76) presents a four-part plan of the creation: thought, music, vision, existence. Another very detailed plan is given by Vramming (1985: 12). Pirson (1998: 71f.) has drawn up a parallel between the plan of creation in Genesis and in the *Ainulindalë*.

[17] Cf. Home V, 156: "Then said Ilúvatar: 'Of the theme that I have declared to you [...] I desire now that ye make in harmony together a great music'". HoME X, 8 has: "I will" and not "I desire", with capitals for Great Music.

out, with Tolkien naming the instruments that play this music: in particular, harps, lutes, flutes and pipes.[18] But what form does the Great Music take? Is it only heard, is it seen, does it exist (that is to say, is it identified with reality)? Christopher Tolkien has drawn attention to the major difference in conception that we encounter here (HoME I, 62; V, 166; X, 25). In versions A and B the Great Music does not pass through the stage of the Vision. Eru has already brought it into existence.

A (and B)	C (C* and D)
'Behold your choiring and your music! *Even* as ye played so of my will your music *took shape*, and lo! *even now* the world unfolds and its history begins.' (HoME I, 55, cf. V 159, emphasis added)	'Behold your music!' And he *showed* to them a *vision*, giving to them *sight* where before was *only hearing*; and they *saw* a new World made *visible* before them. (HoME X, 11, emphasis added)

So the Great Music is made manifest through different senses (hearing, sight)[19] from version C. It is not immediately equivalent to reality.[20] Tolkien makes the revelation or perception of the music progressive: audible, visible, real (i.e. totally perceptible). In a way of speaking, version C takes us from a live concert to a video clip! Armed with these huge differences, we can now enter into the details of the origins. But if the Vision is not original, how is it with the Second Music?

---

[18] See HoME I, 53; V, 156-157; X, 9. Vramming (1985: 21) links this list with the one in Psalm 150: trumpet, psaltery, harp, stringed instruments, organ, cymbals. Giessl (2006) points out that instruments are abandoned in favour of singing from version B; that is to say Tolkien moved from a Latin conception of angel musicians (instrumentalists) to a more Byzantine one (singers). On this point see Lacoste (1984: 563)

[19] For the pre-eminence of these two senses, and particularly the second, see the Platonic reading of Giannone (1984: 175)

[20] On the physical sense of these metaphors see Cough (1999: 5): "We may wonder about the *physics* entailed in creating a Universe, what kind of 'vision' or 'hearing' there could have been *before* the Universe was made, in what way 'mind' might have existed without 'substance'".

2) The second music

From the first version (A-A) on, Tolkien envisages that a Second Music "shall be woven before the seat of Ilúvatar by the choirs of both Ainur and the sons of Men after the Great End" (HoME I, 53).[21] The idea of this Second Music is found again at the end of the text, where Tolkien states that, while Men will join with the Ainur, nothing is known about the destiny of the Elves. Nevertheless, with the first mention of the idea of the Second Music in version B-B, there emerges as a subsequent feature the expression "the choirs of [...] the Children of Ilúvatar", which must include the Elves! Christopher Tolkien has preserved the uncertainty and has avoided coming down on one side or the other (HoME I, 63).[22]

The idea of this second music may recall several things in the Christian tradition. First, the acclaim of the hosts gathered before the throne on the Lamb in Revelations XIX, 1. The second music is certainly that to which mankind is to attain; as Justinian says, man is to become a "second angel, δευτερος αγγελος" (cited in Lacoste 1984: 574). Similarly, in Tolkien the Eruhíni are to become like Valar (HoME IX, 401 and X, 355), which recalls the Gospels: Mark XII, 25, Matthew XXII, 30, and Luke XX, 35-36.

Next, the Second Music may be reminiscent of the *Sanctus* sung in the Mass (from Isaiah VI, 3). This is how it appears in the Mass known as that of St. Pius V: "Through Whom [sc. Jesus Christ] the Angels praise Thy majesty, the Dominations worship it, the Powers stand in awe. The Heavens and the Heavenly hosts together with the blessed Seraphim in triumphant chorus unite to celebrate it. Together with them we entreat Thee, that Thou mayest bid our voices also to be admitted, while we say in lowly praise: *Holy* [...]".[23]

---

[21] Cf. HoME V, 157 and X, 9, 15, where the explicit mention of the 'seat' disappears.

[22] This hesitation is basic to the *Athrabeth*, where we learn that perhaps the Elves will be delivered by Men (HoME X, 319). This hesitation opens the discussion on hope set out by Whittingham (1998: 219f.)

[23] "Per quem majestatem tuam laudant Angeli, adorant Dominationes, tremunt Potestates, Cæli cælorumque Virtutes, ac beata Seraphim, socia exultatione concelebrant. Cum

Finally, the idea developed by Tolkien straight after the mention of the Second Music about the complete comprehension of the intentions of the Creator, each according to his measure,[24] may recall on the one hand the idea of beatitude (everyone is as happy as he can be, i.e. just as a full vase is completely full even if it is small, so everyone will be completely happy according to their individual potential), and on the other the communion of saints, in particular from version B on.[25]

So we have seen from two examples how the category *original* could help us to see which ideas in Tolkien are constant and which undergo a process of evolution. We shall now consider the features that are *subsequent*.

B. Subsequent

1) Bereshith

The opening of the *Ainulindalë* is not original (in the sense of going back to the origin), but subsequent from version B-B on. Tolkien had a tendency to add to it. The very first version (A-A) began "Behold, Ilúvatar dwelt alone" (HoME I, 52). From version A-B he is careful to specify in an introductory sentence (see HoME I, 60, n. 1) that this account is unknown to men, little known to elves, and that Manwë told it to the ancestors of Rúmil. There is the same evolution in version B: in B-A the text begins with " There was Ilúvatar, the All-father, and he made first the Ainur" (HoME V, 156); and version B-B again introduces a (new) introductory sentence specifying that these were the words of Rúmil concerning the "beginning of the World" (HoME V, 156; cf. p. 164, n. 1). This sentence is found again in C, C* and D. But the difficulty in starting was not over, since in D Tolkien added yet another sentence (cf. HoME X, 30)!

---

quibus et nostras voces, ut admitti jubeas, deprecamur, supplici confessione dicentes : *Sanctus* [...]"

[24] "Ainur and Men will know his mind and heart as well as may be, and all his intent" (HoME I, 53).

[25] "[...] all shall understand his intent in their part, and shall know the comprehension each of each" (HoME V, 157, X, 9); cf. "[...] all then understand fully his intent in their part, and each shall know the comprehension of each" (*Silmarillion*, 16).

After all this, we need to remember that the idea of an account of the "beginning of the World" *expressis verbis* is only subsequent, from version B-B.[26] It is found again at the start of the *Valaquenta*: "In the beginning Eru, the One, who in Arda is called Ilúvatar, made the Ainur of his thought" (*Silmarillion* 25).[27] In *The Silmarillion* there is a certain redundancy between the *Ainulindalë* and the *Valaquenta*, since the former text says: "There was Eru, the One, who in Arda is called Ilúvatar, and he made first the Ainur" (p. 15). Two things need to be noted here: first, that the inclusion of the name Eru is a unique feature of the 1977 *Silmarillion*[28]; and second, that the idea of an account of the "beginning of the World" which made the transition between the *Ainulindalë* and the *Valaquenta* has disappeared in this text. From this point on, if, as Randel Helms claims (1981: 25), the beginning of the *Valaquenta* makes a clear allusion to Genesis (because of this use of "beginning"), then this allusion can also apply to the *Ainulindalë*. Besides, Tolkien himself gives as a minimal description of the *Ainulindalë* in the second draft of the letter to Katherine Farrer of 15ᵗʰ June 1948 (?): "'The Music of the Ainur', the Beginning" (HoME X, 5). Now, as everyone knows, that is how Genesis begins: "In the beginning", in Hebrew *Bereshith*. This liminal mention is far from insignificant. Caland (2004: 338) comments on it, emphasizing the linear representation of time: "La cosmogonie tolkienienne postule aussi un commencement et une fin. La linéarité est donc

---

[26] Which beginning of *the world* is it anyway? Tolkien sometimes seems to be thinking of a world actually in existence, as when the wise speak of the rebellion of Melkor in the music of the Ainur before the "beginning" (HoME X, 74, § 45 (cf. p. 409), cf. p.110, § 127; see also HoME XII, 420, n. 10). See also HoME X, 378, where the "regions of the Beginning" refers to a time after the *fiat* of Eä.

[27] At the origin of the *Valaquenta* stands "After the making of the World by the Allfather, who in elvish tongue is names Ilúvatar" (HoME IV, 78). In other words, the text starts not with the idea of "beginning" but with events subsequent ("after") to the creation. This form of the *Valaquenta* did not begin with a résumé from zero of the *Ainulindalë*; that dates only from December 1937-January 1938 (cf. HoME V, 204, and p. 20 for the dating), when it is known that version B-B of the *Ainulindalë* was already in existence (see HoME V, 207, §1; cf. p. 165, n. 20). The Annals of Valinor open with the idea that in the beginning Ilúvatar "made all things" and that the Valar "came into the World" (HoME IV, 263; V, 110); the Annals of Aman replace "all things" by "Eä" (HoME X, 48).

[28] On the difference fo meaning between Eru and Ilúvatar, see Flieger (1986: 129f.).

respectée, l'univers créé s'inscrivant avant le nôtre. Tout concorde une fois de plus vers le "faire croire", sans heurter la religion chrétienne, tout au plus en la complétant".[29] Norse mythology, on the contrary, has no concept of temporality and history (see Boyer 1987: 121).

The idea of the "beginning of the World" is therefore not present from the start in those precise words; it is a subsequent feature from the second version on, where Tolkien wrote over the opening of his text. Nevertheless the topic is a weighty and important one. What is to be said about that other well-known term: "*Eä!*"?

2) *Eä!*

The term *Eä* is perhaps the best known in the *Ainulindalë*. Verlyn Flieger (2002: 58ff.) has even suggested that all Tolkien does is explore the word *Eä*.[30] Indeed, the term signifies the creation as a unique act of bringing into being by God and its result: "All Creation" (HoME XI, 402), in the sense of the world around us. It is undoubtedly the richness of the Quenya invented by Tolkien which makes this *Eä* so special. In fact, "en quenya, Eä est à la fois l'infinitif du verbe être, exister, le présent du mode impératif (« soit ! » ou « existe ») et l'univers au sens théologique [...] Loin des cosmogonies nordiques ou grecques, la référence choisie est limpide. 'Dieu dit: "Que la lumière soit!" Et la lumière fut' (Caland 2004: 342).[31] Indeed, "l'élément le

---

[29] 'The Tolkienian cosmogony also postulates a beginning and an end. Therefore linearity is respected, with the created universe inscribing itself before our own. Once again everything comes together to "create belief", without detracting from the Christian religion, but rather completing it.'

[30] Similarly, according to Simonne d'Ardenne (1975: 10) Tolkien is one of those "qui ont compris toute la valeur de la phrase biblique" ('who understood the whole weight of the Biblical phrase').

[31] 'in Quenya, Eä is at the same time the infinitive of the verb *to be*, *exist*, the present of the imperative mood (*be!* or *exist!*) and the universe in the theological sense [...] Quite unlike the Norse or Greek cosmogonies, the chosen reference is transparent. "God said: Let there be light.' And there was light".' Cf. Kloczko (1995: 42a). Caldecott (2003: 76) points out that it is also the first word of creation according to the Koran: *kun*, be!

plus original du texte de la *Genèse* est évidemment que Dieu produit tous les êtres par la seule émission de sa Parole" (Bouyer 1982: 85).[32]

The allusion is so self-evident that anyone would think it had always been there. How is it possible to imagine an account of the creation without the creator's word? But in the *Book of Lost Tales* there is no *Eä!* This equivalent of the *fiat* is actually subsequent, from version C on. Therefore Eru's words "Let these things Be" date only from 1948. The Elvish word *Eä* itself, the strict equivalent of the use of the Latin *fiat* in a French or English sentence (since Quenya is the Latin of the Elves) appears only in version D, that is to say between 1948 and 1951 (HoME X, 31).

Nevertheless there are some differences between Tolkien's *Eä* and the *fiat* of the Old Testament. By St. Augustine, for example, *fiat lux* is interpreted as the creation of the angels.[33] In Tolkien, *Eä* is certainly the creation of the world. Furthermore, in Genesis the world is created good: God saw that it was good. In Tolkien, evil exists before *Eä* is pronounced (*Letters*, 286). As in a good theodicy, evil in Tolkien is overdetermined by good.[34]

If the beginning was subsequent from the second version on (but nevertheless early), *Eä* itself is subsequent from the last version. Some Catholic elements were added early on, while others came only at a very late stage. Let us now see which features can be regarded as *unique*.

---

[32] 'the most original element in the Genesis text is that God produces the whole of being simply by uttering His Word'. On the friendly relations between Bouyer and Tolkien, see Devaux (2003b), an English version of which, translated by Jean-Yves Lacoste, will appear in the proceedings of the Oxford Tolkien Conference, Exeter College, August 2006.

[33] On this point see Houghton (2002: 175), who explains that when God said *fiat*, that means the creation of things as ideas, while the *fuit* marks the actual creation of these ideas in the minds of the angels. The *fiat lux* refers to the creation of the angels themselves.

[34] See Houghton (2002: 179f.) and Whittingham (1998: 216). For the opposite view, see Giessl (2006), who argues that Melkor corrupted the themes, so that not only beneficial effects can be seen in them.

C. Unique

1) The divine song of creation, first version

In version A, right at the end we come across two unique features. First, Ilúvatar "sang into being the Ainur" (HoME X, 52)! This idea belongs to this version alone; here Ilúvatar begins by singing, whereas in all the other versions he speaks, and only the Ainur sing. After that, and again only here, Tolkien develops the first activities of the Ainur: Ilúvatar teaches them "all manner of things", beginning with music (HoME I, 52). Therefore the music of the Ainur comes from Ilúvatar, not only the theme of the music (the Design), but also the faculty of musicianship. The music of the Ainur, the musicality of the Ainur becomes innate in them only when it seems to be self-evident that they are musicians from version B on.

The difference between a sung creation and a spoken creation of the Ainur by Ilúvatar is not negligible in its theological consequences. In fact, as Carla Giannone (1984: 169) has shown, in the 1977 *Ainulindalë* (and indeed from version B on), Tolkien distinguishes two hierarchical levels, God and the gods (Eru Ilúvatar and the Ainur) as a function of this difference between speech and song.[35] Strictly speaking, there is no music played by Eru.[36] God's prerogative (and his act of creation) resides in the Λογος ("In the beginning was the Word", says the prologue to St. John's Gospel), which is also thought. It is not for nothing that in version B the Ainur become "the offspring of his thought" (HoME V, 156). This is the explanation for the replacement of the idea of a sung creation: for "sang" is substituted the more indeterminate "made"; or rather, its determination or precision consists in saying that the Ainur are the "offspring" of the thought of Ilúvatar. Two problems are present here: is "make" equivalent to "create", and does the

---

[35] "Tolkien accentua la distinzione tra i due anche a livelo segnico quando scrive che Ilúvatar *spoke* e gli Ainur *sang*" ('Tolkien stresses the distinction between the two levels on the level of signs too, when he writes that Ilúvatar *spoke* and the Ainur *sang*').

[36] In a note Tolkien uses the expression "Music of Eru" (HoME X, 327), but it is not stated explicitly that Eru is playing.

word "offspring" authorise us to think that Tolkien has recourse to a doctrine of emanation?

Tolkien himself was careful to distinguish between the two in the draft of a letter to Peter Hastings of September 1954 (*Letters*, 190 fn.): "Inside this mythical history (as its metaphysic is [...]) Creation, the act of Will of Eru the One that gives Reality to conceptions, is distinguished from Making, which is permissive". But surely giving Reality to conceptions what happens with the "offspring of his thought" who defined the Making, while in the letter that is the definition of creation. The fact that the problem of a theodicy arises (permitting evil in the creation) should not make any difference. The confusion is created by the initial use of "make" as applied to the Ainur. Perhaps Tolkien would have corrected this "made" to a clear "created" if he had returned to the *Ainulindalë* after 1954. We may gain some hints on this question by considering the second problem, which revolves not around the first term ("made") but around its gloss ("offspring").

Is it a question of Neoplatonic emanation? Flieger (2002:51; 1986: 130) has argued to this effect, while a similar position is taken by Giannone (1984: 168f.). DiNapoli (1997: 28b) would not take emanation back to this point, but he begins to see it from the incarnation of the Valar on. However, according to Houghton (2002: 182) and Irigaray (1999: 43), the answer must be in the negative. The latter takes his argument from two letters of 1958 and 1964 (that is to say after the final version of 1954), which specifically state that the Ainur are "created" and "angelical first-created" (*Letters*, 284, 245). So there we also have an answer to our first question.

At the end of this inquiry into the various 'origins', we are in a position to recognise the evolutions hidden in a passage from version A: "those things that ye have sung and played, lo! I have caused to be – not in the musics that ye make in the heavenly regions, as a joy to me and a play unto yourselves, alone, but rather to have shape and reality even as have ye Ainur [...]. Maybe I shall love these things that come of my thought even as I love the Ainur who are of my song" (Home I, 54-55, cf. V, 158). Three unique features are found here: Ilúvatar sings ("my song"), the Ainur are sung by him,[37] and he has already caused the world, with or without the vision. In the definitive version, Ilúvatar does not sing, the Ainur are the offspring of his thought (and not of his song), and Ilúvatar shows them the world as a vision before he says *Eä*.[38]

2) A fundamentally different unique version (C*)

At the top of the version C* typescript is written "Round World Version", and on B-B/C "Old Flat World Version"(HoME X, 4).[39] Tolkien undoubtedly made this distinction at the time when he wrote to Katherine Farrer on 15th June 1948 (*Letters*, 130; draft in HoME X, 5). According to Christopher Tolkien, the "Flat World Version" applies to version B-B, before the emendations of C, or to put it another way, version C takes into account the advice of Katherine Farrer, who preferred the "Flat World Version". So Tolkien returned to this manuscript, restoring and modifying what he had already changed in C*; that is the genesis of version C.[40]

This version contains elements which are entirely unique, so much so that the whole nature of certain conceptions is changed. The world as it is now conceived is *fundamentally* different.[41] Some commentators even think that this version is no longer based on the mythology (Apeland 1998: 46). Even if certain elements are whimsical, such as when the origin of the moon is explained by the battle against the malice of Melkor (HoME X, 42), nevertheless the most important and decisive aspect of this story is that the

---

[37] This unique feature is already altered in version A-B; see HoME I, 60, n. 4.

[38] The intervention of the vision is most marked in version C (where the other points disappear): "I will show them [sc. those things that the Ainur have sung] that ye may see what ye have done" (HoME X, 10, §9). The opposition between "I have caused to be" and "I will show" is maximal; it is greatly strengthened by the verb tenses.

[39] Concerning the *Flat World*, see also HoME X, 270.

[40] See HoME X, 6, and cf. Noad (2000: 51f, 59).

[41] For what I call a "fundamental" change, Christopher Tolkien uses the expressions "wholly divergent in essential respects" (HoME X, 3), "radical changes in the structure" (7), or "radical re-ordering" (23). But if the difference between B and C is described in these terms, that between C and C* is even greater: "a much more radical – one might say a devastating – change in the cosmology" (HoME X, 3).

moon and the sun do not hark back nostalgically to the Trees, because in this 'scientifically correct' version they have always been there.[42] The world is *not at all* the same.

III. CATHOLIC ELEMENTS

Among the commentaries devoted to the *Ainulindalë*, only one tackles head on the question of the 'matter of the North': that of John Cough (1999: 7). Referring to the prose Edda of Snorri Sturluson, he emphasizes that in the Norse myth there is no creation *ex nihilo* since everything comes from Yggdrasil, and he concludes that "the Norse myth and Tolkien's clearly share no common ground". The relationship is "superficial".[43] Other articles have claimed more or less strongly the possible similarities to Sumerian, Hindu,[44] Egyptian or Vedic[45] traditions. But even if some have said that the name *Ainulindalë* is reminiscent of the *Kalevala* (Cough 1999: 5), it is principally with the Christian account in Genesis that the *Ainulindalë* is compared.[46]

Finding the exact word to express this relationship is something of a poser! The *Ainulindalë* is presented in the *Histoire chrétienne de la littérature* as the "[récit] imperturbabl[e d']une autre création du monde et de

---

[42] Cf. Giessl's (2006) insistence on this point. Concerning the relationship of the two Trees to the fundamental cosmological ideas of version C*, see Scull (2000: 15).

[43] On Norse cosmology see Boyer (1981), Chapter VIII. Caland (2004: 334) sees a comparison between "The Music of the Ainur" in *The Book of Lost Tales* and the *Gylfaginning* in the prose Edda because they are dialogues. This similarity leads her to think that version A is "largely inspired by the Norse *Gylfaginning*". According to her, the vision of the world as a drakkar is comparable to Yggdrasil (p. 335). For Bonnal (1998: 45) the ice and fire wielded by Melkor are the two forces which allow a comparison with Norse mythology. Similarly, the comparison is justified by the feminine gender of the sun and masculine of the moon in Tolkien (p. 46).

[44] See Vramming (1985), and the comparison with Paramahansa Yogananda, *Autobiographie d'un Yogi* (Paris: Adyar, 2003) by Davis (1982: 7f.) (the distinction between the Design, the Vision and the Achievement corresponding to that between the three kingdoms, causal, astral and physical).

[45] Giannone (1984: 170)

[46] The first version of the *Ainulindalë* (1918-20) does not appear to owe anything to Tolkien's reading of Genesis in Old English, since he did not do that until Wednesday 20th October 1920 if we are to believe his personal copy preserved in Oxford.

l'homme, *parallèle*, mais non parodique, à celle de la Bible" (Peny 1996: 1020, emphasis added).[47] As Caland (2004: 338) puts it, "il n'est pas question pour Tolkien, bien entendu, de réécrire la Bible",[48] he is "completing" the Christian religion. For Caldecott (2003: 74), Tolkien's account is "complementary" to the Genesis story. After a quotation from the *Ainulindalë*, Dufayet (2003: 206) writes: "Le *Silmarillion* est le texte le plus explicitement *analogique* à la Bible et à la pensée chrétienne de la création, puisque le monde 'secondaire' (comme le 'monde primaire') a été créé *ex nihilo* par un acte de volonté de l'Unique".[49] According to Shippey (1992: 209), it is a calque on Genesis and Milton's *Paradise Lost*, as well as on St. Augustine. Bellet (internet) stresses the echoes of the King James Version in the archaising style of Tolkien's text. Cough (1999: 3) speaks of deliberate compatibility, while for Pearce (1998: 84) the appropriate expression would be "remarkable similarity". Pirson (1998: 70) has put the argument from the negative side: there is no formal contradiction between the *Ainulindalë* and Genesis.

Parallel but non-parodistic, completion, complementarity, analogy, calque, deliberate compatibility, remarkable similarity, absence of formal contradiction: the commentators have not lacked vocabulary to express the relationship between the *Ainulindalë* and Genesis. In *Letters* 131 Tolkien speaks of the Ainur as gods that can be accepted "by a mind that believes in the Blessed Trinity" (p. 146). This notion of acceptability can no doubt be extended to the *Ainulindalë*. From an internal point of view this acceptability is translated, literally, by the adaptation to our intellectual powers and our languages. In fact Tolkien specifies that if the *Ainulindalë* was known in

---

[47] 'Imperturbable account of a different creation of the world and of man, parallel to, but not parodying, that of the Bible.'

[48] 'Of course, for Tolkien there is no question of re-writing the Bible.'

[49] 'The *Silmarillion* is the most explicitly analogical text to the Bible and to Christian thinking about the creation, since the "secondary" world (like the "primary world") was created *ex nihilo* by an act of will of the One'. Caland also speaks of a (Judaeo-)Christian model. The *Ainulindalë* is also presented as the "reflet mimétique" ('mimetic reflection') of Genesis (p. 207). For Davis (1982: 6a) on the other hand, there are both biblical and eddaic origins, but it is "mere mimesis".

Rúmil's Quenya version,[50] it must have been told by the Aratar (no doubt Manwë) in that language "according to our modes of thought and our imagination of the visible world, in symbols that were intelligible to us".[51]

If this acceptability is extended, it may be useful to read Richard Purtill (1984: 119-133); his summary of the differences between traditional Catholic theology and that of the *Ainulindalë* and the *Valaquenta* clearly sets out the limits of the comparison. He notes three main differences in the *Ainulindalë*: a part of the creation is the work of the angels; these angels are material; and the created world is always perverted or marred since the malice of Melkor interfered in its making. Two other major differences are made clear in the *Valaquenta*: the angels are male and female (and can marry), and Melkor is the first to fall (whereas in Catholic theology the fallen angels all fall simultaneously).[52] Finally, Purtill emphasizes that Tolkien's intention was not to re-write Genesis nor to interpret it, but to create a myth (p. 132). Undoubtedly it has to be seen from both sides, proximity and distance. If there were no difference, we would not ask ourselves the question. The important thing is to know how far the resemblance goes and whether the points of divergence are secondary or not. I shall concentrate on three main points: the creator, the sub-creators, and the one who introduces evil.[53]

---

[50] Irigaray (1999: 27) emphasizes the editorial gap (and even error) created by the omission in the 1977 *Silmarillion* of the complete title as found for example in HoME X, 30: "error en la forma en que decidió editarlo [...] los restos de una antigua tradición sapiencial, y como tales no eran *omniscientes ni infalibles*" ('error in the form in which he decided to edit it [...] the remains of an ancient tradition of wisdom, and as such were neither omniscient nor infallible'). See also the remarks by Giessl (2006) concerning the characters who transmit the legends, and also Garnier (2003).

[51] HoME XI, 406-407. In HoME X, 370 Tolkien thinks that the cosmological account has come down to us in a Mannish form, and that the Elves knew the truth "according to their measure of understanding". According to Caldecott (2003: 74) the difference from the Genesis account is explained by the transmission of the legends, which come from the Noldor and reach us via Hobbits.

[52] Purtill also maintains that a *creation* through music is not Christian (p. 120). But if music has a supernatural power in the *Kalevala* (see for example Garth 2003: 254), nevertheless this idea is also found in the Bible (Job XXXVIII, 7). The idea is also medieval, as in the music of the spheres (see Eden 2002). Timmons (1998: 61) criticises Purtill's approach.

[53] On the last two points I would like to take the opportunity to point out the sensitive investigation being carried out by Jean-Philippe Qadri into the ternary structures in

A. Eru Ilúvatar, the "transcendental creator"

Is the idea of a transcendental creator necessarily associated with Eru Ilúvatar? According to Cough (1999: 7), "Behind the Norse myth, the only ultimate power or agent, which might correspond to Eru, the One, is Fate, or in Old English, Wyrd".[54] Is this identification the most appropriate one? Should we not rather turn to Christianity? Is it not the idea of creation *ex nihilo*, above all else, which brings the *Ainulindalë* close to Genesis? As Caland 2004: 337) says, " Excepté dans la mythologie mésopotamienne, le dieu suprême des grandes mythologies n'est jamais le créateur de l'univers, comme le souligne A.H. Krappe".[55]

It is certainly this idea of a creator, and indeed of a transcendental creator, that Tolkien insists on in his letter to Christopher Bretherton of 16th July 1964 (*Letters*, p. 345): "In O[xford] I wrote a cosmogonical myth, 'The Music of the Ainur', defining the relation of The One, the transcendental Creator, to the Valar, the 'Powers', the angelical First-created, and their plan in ordering and carrying out the Primeval Design. It was also told how it came about that Eru, the One, made an addition to the Design: introducing the themes of the Eruhîn, the Children of God, The Firstborn (Elves) and the Successors (Men), whom the Valar were forbidden to try and dominate by fear or force".[56]

Ilúvatar is then the creator of everything, *ex nihilo*. How does this creation begin? In the Bible, God first creates the heavens, the earth and the waters. In the *Ainulindalë*, Eru first creates the Ainur, the void in which they are, and the music. Caldecott (2003: 74, 77) has shown what correspondence could exist between these three creations in the two accounts.

Tolkien's narrative and the match between background and form (Internet, see References).

[54] Cough also mentions the other figures of impersonal destiny, Muslim (*kismet*) or Greek (*ananke*).

[55] 'Except in Mesopotamian mythology, the supreme god of the great mythologies is never the creator of the universe, as is stressed by A. H. Krappe'. The reference is to Krappe's *La Genèse des Mythes*.

[56] On the justification for the expression "cosmogonical myth", see Ciceri (1995).

B. The Ainur as sub-creators

1) The Creator and the sub-creators

The difference between Ilúvatar and the Ainur[57] can be marked in various ways. First, as Tolkien says, strictly speaking the creation is the work of God while the making is given over to the Valar (*Letters*, p.190 fn.). Then, as we have seen, Ilúvatar speaks and the Ainur sing (Giannone 1984: 169). There is no originality here on Tolkien's part as against the Catholic tradition; the association of the angels with music is an important theme in that tradition (see Lacoste 1984). Certainly Tolkien insists more than St. Augustine on music, while St. Augustine insists more on words and light (Houghton 2002: 178f.). Finally, Marjorie Burns (1998: 9) has remarked on the difference between the Ainur conceived as Gods, then as those that men call Gods, and finally as gods with a small letter, just as she has pointed out the abandonment of an excessively marked gender ("wife" becomes "spouse"). That is as much as to say that in this respect Tolkien made his text more acceptable in a Catholic context.[58]

I have explored elsewhere (Devaux 2003c) the correspondence between the hierarchies of angels in the Church Fathers and the Aratar, Valar and Maiar in Tolkien. It is sufficient here to recall that the angels or the pantheon are not chaotic; the Valar do not occur at random. There exist a clear hierarchy and marked attributes.[59]

Assuming that the idea of angelic music causes no problems and a theologisation has taken place, what is there to be said about this music as sub-creative?[60] Father Robert Murray (1998: 51, n. 12) reports that in a conversation, Tolkien once told him that in his opinion the angels had played

---

[57] Tolkien varied the number of great Valar (the Aratar); there were only four originally (HoME I, 9).

[58] The female nature of the Valier is compared with the importance of female saints in Catholic tradition by Garbowski (2004: 114).

[59] This is in distinction to the Norse pantheon; on this point see Boyer (1987: 121).

[60] The angels are the sub-creators of Arda from an internal point of view, while Tolkien also describes himself as a sub-creator, but from a point of view external to the world he creates. For the vocabulary of sub-creation, see Dufayet (2003: 206).

a large part in the creation. Fr. Murray had taken that as his stance on "Catholic" theology, since he had not yet seen *The Silmarillion,* whereas Tolkien was really talking about his secondary world. C. S. Lewis (1964: 121) also said that the sublunary world was not made directly, but its elements were made by secondary agents.[61] Tolkien's Ainur are certainly more sub-creative than Augustine's angels, but of course Augustine was rebutting the Manichaeans, who granted a large role to sub-creators (see Houghton 2002: 179f.). Nevertheless, in Catholic doctrine the angels certainly play some part in the construction and administration of the creation.[62] "In giving the Ainur power to create, Ilúvatar has not reduced his own creative force; he has simply extended it, including their efforts within his own" (Whittingham 1998: 216). So what is novel in Tolkien is the way in which he makes two Christian themes coincide: the musical angels on one side, and their sub-creation on the other. There is also a second point in which the Ainur particularly resemble the Catholic angels: their knowledge.

2) Morning and evening knowledge

Theology distinguishes between two kinds of angelic knowledge: that of the morning and that of the evening (see Cessario 2000, 41-45). "C'est s. Augustin qui a introduit cette distinction de la connaissance angélique [...]. Il appelle connaissance du matin celle de l'être primordial des choses, connaissance qui porte sur les choses selon qu'elles sont dans le Verbe; tandis qu'il appelle connaissance du soir la connaissance de l'être créé comme existant dans sa nature propre".[63] To perceive the Word, before the creation, is precisely the situation which the Music has made possible for the

---

[61] Caldecott (2003: 75) reminds us that Lewis made Aslan sing Narnia into being.

[62] See Caldecott (2003: 80f.) for the relationship to the latest Catechism of the Catholic Church. Pirson (1998: 58, n. 6) refers to the Book of Job on this question. This tradition is more Catholic than Protestant; see Garbowski (2004: 115).

[63] 'It was St. Augustine who introduced this distinction in angelic knowledge [...]. He calls *morning knowledge* that of the primordial being of things, knowledge related to things as they are in the Word ; while he calls *evening knowledge* the knowledge of the created being as existing in its own nature.' St. Thomas Aquinas, *Summa Theologiae,* Ia p., qu. 58, art. 6, rep. Cf. Houghton (2002: 175).

Ainur. But there are elements that the Valar discover only in the course of History. So what knowledge is it that the Valar lack?

Let us listen to the music again. The idea of its developing according to three themes is original. After the first theme Ilúvatar raises his right hand, then after the second theme his left hand, and finally after the third theme he raises both together. Like a conductor, Ilúvatar raises his hands and the themes change. Another original feature is the idea of the Valar not having complete knowledge of the music.[64] We can find an example of incompleteness in their morning knowledge. It is known that the Children of Ilúvatar appear in the third theme and that they come from Ilúvatar alone, since the Valar have played no part in their creation. It is significant that what the Valar do *not* know in relation to the Eruhíni concerns their destiny. Fornet-Ponse (2005: 158-166) explains how the music establishes only the main outlines of history, and that since the Elves live throughout time, they are partly bound by the music, which is not the case with Men, being mortal and ephemeral (cf. HoME V, 247). Therefore the Valar cannot know through morning knowledge what is going to happen to Men. But the same is true of Elves. This the death of Míriel poses a problem for the Valar, who even when gathered in conclave do not know what to do and therefore refer the matter to Ilúvatar.[65]

C. The fall of the greatest of the Ainur and Lucifer

1) The fall of Melkor

The similarities between Melkor and the devil[66], Satan or Lucifer are very widely drawn. Of course Melkor is considered as the greatest of the angels, the one who has fallen, just as in the Catholic tradition. Nevertheless, it is

---

[64] See for version A: HoME I, 57 (their knowledge is "incomplete", some elements of the future are "unforeseen"); B : HoME V, 160 ("unforeseen"); C (therefore also C* and D): HoME X, 11 ("unseen"). The paragraphs where this idea occurs are not parallel between A-B and C-C*-D.

[65] On this point see the whole collection on the reincarnation of the Elves edited and with an introduction by me (Devaux 2007).

[66] Tolkien calls him "Diabolus": (HoME X, 412; *Letters* p. 195).

possible to identify differences between the fall of Melkor and that of Lucifer (see Purtill 2003: 128ff. and Schweicher (1995). Tolkien came to consider Melkor as the greatest of the angels.[67] Is he then the equivalent of one of the seraphim, of whom St. Bernard of Clairvaux, for example, said that they are "the fire of God"?[68] As a unique feature, only version B-A dares to write that before his fall Melkor was seated "upon the left hand of Ilúvatar" (HoME V, 163, n. 3). It is notable that this is the exact opposite of the place taken by Jesus Christ in the Catholic tradition, as is taught by the sixth article of faith in the Apostles' Creed.[69]

2) Melkor and the secret Fire

Giannone (1984: 172f.) has clearly identified the difference between Melkor and Lucifer. The Arata is associated with heat more than light; his desire for the Imperishable Flame "grew hot" within him, and malice "burned" in him. In the end he even takes on that form: his eyes are "like a flame that withers with heat and pierces with a deadly cold" (*Silmarillion*, 22)! Melkor is a synthesis of negative elements, water, air, earth and fire, but he lacks the light of Ilúvatar. Physically, the hotter a flame is, the less light it gives.[70]

---

[67] In version A he has "*some* of the greatest gifts of power and wisdom and knowledge" (HoME I 53, emphasis added); in version B-A that becomes "*many* of the greatest gifts of power and knowledge" (HoME V, 164, n. 4, emphasis added), then in B-B "*the greatest* gifts of power and knowledge" (HoME V, 157, emphasis added). On the evolution of his power, see Giessl (2006: 157-164).

[68] *De Consideratione*, book V, §11. If Sauron were not of a lower order, it would be tempting to see in him a fallen Cherub, since it is by the intermediary effect of the Cherubim that God 'is all eye, and an infallible eye, since it is never closed; he has no need of any light to see other than his own, being eye and light both together' (V, §10). But the Seraphim and Cherubim are held, as for example by Dionysius the Areopagite (in *De Cælesti hierarchia*), to be of the same rank, while the angels are inferior to them, in the same way that the Maiar (including Sauron) are inferior to the Aratar (Melkor).

[69] "Le 'à la droite' exprime l'honneur qui est rendu a cette nature" ('The "at the right hand" expresses the honour which is given to this nature') (Balthasar 1992: 79).

[70] The flame that animates Melkor also characterises the Balrogs. They can be compared with the dragon of hell in the visions of St. Frances of Rome.

What Melkor lacks is the secret Fire. This is known to be a reference to the Holy Spirit, as Tolkien said to C. S. Kilby (1977: 59).[71] In version A-A the secret fire is a *hapax* whose internal signification is 'giving life and reality'. In version A-B it occurs twice more.[72] The secret Fire "dwelleth with Ilúvatar" (HoME I, 54), just like the Word which was with God and which was God (according to the Prologue to St. John's Gospel). The secret Fire will be given to everyone after the end of time (§4). Like the Word, the third person of the Trinity is with God. This is confirmed by Tolkien when he refers to the meaning of the secret Fire or the Imperishable Flame[73] of the *Ainulindalë* in the Notes to the Commentary on the *Athrabeth*:

> " [...] in the *Ainulindalë*, in which reference is made to the 'Flame Imperishable'. This appears to mean the Creative activity of Eru (in some sense distinct from or within Him), by which things could be given a 'real' and independent (though derivative and created) existence. The Flame Imperishable is sent out from Eru, to dwell in the heart of the world, and the world then Is, on the same plane as the Ainur, and they can enter into it. But this is not, of course, the same as the re-entry of Eru to defeat Melkor. It refers rather to the mystery of 'authorship', by which the author, while remaining 'outside' and independent of his work, also 'indwells' in it, on its derivative plane, below that of his own being, as the source and guarantee of its being".
> (HoME X, 345, n. 11)

Here Tolkien provides a place for the Trinity. The secret Fire, the Holy Spirit, is "distinct from or within Him", just as the One God is three and one

---

[71] The origin of the Fire as Holy Spirit is found in the *Qenya Lexicon* (Tolkien 1998: 81), s.v. *Saba*, where Tolkien gives for *Sá*: "Fire, especially in temples, etc. A mystic name identified with Holy Ghost".

[72] See HoME I, 60, n. 2 : "The reference to the setting of the Secret Fire within the Ainur is lacking in the draft"; cf. n. 3.

[73] A subsequent expression from version C on (HoME X, 8).

at the same time. Also the entry and re-entry of Eru[74] find an echo in the Incarnation and the second coming of Jesus. Tolkien after all designed his myth so as to be acceptable to a mind which believes in the Holy Trinity.

What conclusions does this inquiry into the origins of the *Ainulindalë* allow us to draw concerning the catholicity or the catholicisation of the text? We have seen that a number of elements present in it, which I have listed in detail, are "compatible with Catholicism" (Cough 1999: 3). The main points are undoubtedly the following: the idea of creation (1) *ex nihilo* (2) by the word (3) of a creator God; (4) the idea of a second music uniting the choirs of the children of God and the angels; furthermore (5) the idea of the participation of the angels in the creation of the world, and (6) the idea of the fall of the greatest of the angels, and finally (7) even the idea of a Holy Spirit distinct from God but also in Him. If the *final* result, as the redundant expression has it, is acceptable, what about the other versions? We have seen the construction of an *explicit* theologisation of the *legendarium*, notably with the addition of the very Old Testament-like *Eä*. But right from its origins, perhaps more than any other text (although this remains to be verified), the creation according the *Ainulindalë* is acceptable to the Catholic faith.[75]

(Translated from French by Allan Turner)

---

[74] See HoME X, 321 and 345. Cf. Kilby (1977: 62), who speaks of these texts from the *Athrabeth* using these terms: "Christ's incarnation [...] and the final consummation at Christ's return".

[75] I would like to express my gratitude to Philippe Garnier and Thomas Honegger for their contributions towards improving this article.

MICHAËL DEVAUX was born in 1971 and is a Doctor of Philosophy. In 1995 he founded the French Tolkien Society, "La Compagnie de la Comté". He is editor of the journal *La Feuille de la Compagnie* (published by Ad Solem, Geneva). His articles on Tolkien are chiefly concerned with the philosophical and theological aspects of his works (for example death, and the conception of the angels or Valar). He has also translated the whole of *Letters* no. 131, and edited and translated unpublished texts by Tolkien about Elvish reincarnation. He teaches philosophy of education at the Institut Universitaire de Formation de Maîtres de Basse-Normandie.

References

Agøy, Nils Ivar (ed.), 1998a, *Between Faith and Fiction. Tolkien and the Powers of His World*, Proceedings of the Arda Symposium at the Second Northern Tolkien Festival, Oslo, August 1997 (Arda Special 1), Oslo: Arthedain (The Tolkien Society of Norway) / Arda-sällskapet (The Arda-society).

——, 1998b, 'The Fall and Man's Mortality: An Investigation of Some Theological Themes in J. R. R. Tolkien's *Athrabeth Finrod ah Andreth*', in Agøy 1998a, pp. 16-27.

Apeland, Kaj André, 1998, 'On Entering the Same River Twice: Mythology and Theology in the Silmarillion corpus', in Agøy 1998a, pp. 44-50.

d'Ardenne, Simonne, 1975, 'Au commencement était le *Verbe*, et le *Verbe* était avec Dieu, et le *Verbe* était Dieu' (Introduction to *Maître Gilles de Ham (première version)*), Liège: Association des Romanistes de l'Université de Liège.

Balthasar, Hans Urs von, 1992, *Credo. Méditations sur le Symbole des Apôtres*, French translation by. J. Doré & Ch. Flamant, Paris: Nouvelle Cité.

Bellet, Bertrand, 'Style et traduction: l'exemple de l'*Ainulindalë*', work in progress, <http://www.jrrvf.com/forum/noncgi/Forum11/HTML/000152.html>, since 2nd March 2003).

Bonnal, Nicolas, 1998, *Les Univers d'un magicien*, Paris: Les Belles Lettres.

Bouyer, Louis, 1982, *Cosmos. Le Monde et la gloire de Dieu*, Paris: Cerf.

Boyer, Régis, 1987, *Le Christ des Barbares. Le monde nordique (IXe-XIIIe siècles)*, Paris Cerf.

Burns, Marjorie, 1998, "All in One, One in All", in Agøy 1998a, pp. 2-12.

Caldecott, Stratford, 2003, *Secret Fire. The Spiritual Vision of J. R. R. Tolkien*, London: Darton, Longman and Todd.

Caland, Fabienne Claire, 2004, 'La naissance du monde selon J. R. R. Tolkien', in Aline Le Berre (ed.), *De Prométhée à la machine à vapeur: cosmogonie et mythes fondateurs à travers le temps et l'espace* (Espaces humains 8), Limoges: Pulim, pp. 333-356.

Carpenter, Humphrey (ed.), 1981, *The Letters of J. R. R. Tolkien*, London: George Allen and Unwin.

Ciceri, Fabricio, 1995, 'La Musica degli Ainur: un mito cosmogonico', in *Terra di Mezzo*, 1, pp. 24-27.

Cough, John, 1999, 'Tolkien's Creation Myth in *The Silmarillion* – Northern or not?', in *Children's Literature in Education*, 30, 1, pp. 1-8.

Davis, Howard, 1982, 'The *Ainulindalë*: Music of Creation', *Mythlore*, 32, summer, pp. 6-10.

Devaux, Michaël (ed.), 2003a, *Tolkien, les racines du légendaire* (*La Feuille de la Compagnie*, No. 2), Geneva: Ad Solem.

——, 2003b, 'Louis Bouyer & J. R. R. Tolkien: une amitié d'écrivains', in Devaux 2003a, pp. 85-146.

——, 2003c, 'Les anges de l'Ombre chez Tolkien: chair, corps et corruption', in Devaux 2003a, pp.191-245.

——, 2004, 'Rétablir le mythe. Le statut des textes de *L'Histoire de la Terre du Milieu*', in Vincent Ferré (ed.), *Tolkien, trente ans après (1973-2003)*, Paris: Christian Bourgeois, pp.161-188.

——, 2007, *Tolkien, l'effigie des elfes*, Genève: Ad Solem.

DiNapoli, Robert, 2000, 'The Valar and Byzantium. Visions of Hierarchical Splendour in Charles Williams and J. R. R. Tolkien', in Maria Kuteeva (ed.), *The Ways of Creative Mythologies. Imagined Worlds and Their Makers*, Vol. II, Telford: The Tolkien Society, pp. 25-30.

Dufayet, Nathalie, 2003, 'La notion de "création continuée" chez J. R. R. Tolkien', in *Otrante. Arts et littérature fantastique*, No. 14, automne, pp.201-214.

Eden, Bradford Lee, 2002, 'The "music of the spheres". Relationships between Tolkien's *The Silmarillion* and medieval cosmological and religious theory', in Jane Chance (ed.), *Tolkien the Medievalist*, London: Routledge, pp. 183-193.

Flieger, Verlyn, 1986, 'Naming the Unnameable: The Neoplatonic "One" in Tolkien's *Silmarillion*', in Thomas Halton & Joseph P. William (eds.), *Diakonia: studies in honour of Robert I. Meyer*, Washington D. C.: The Catholic University of America Press, pp. 129-130.

——, 2002, *Splintered Light. Logos and Language in Tolkien's World*, revised edition, Kent & London: The Kent State University Press.

Fornet-Ponse, Thomas, 2005 '"In the webs of fate": Freiheit und Determination in der *Ainulindalë* und der *Narn*', *Inklings-Jahrbuch*, Band 23, pp. 153-179.

Garbowski, Christopher, '*The Silmarillion* and *Genesis*: The Contemporary Artist and the Present Revelation, *Annales Universitatis Mariae Curie-Skłodowska: sectio FF*, Lublin (Poland), Vol. XVI, 1998, (available online at <http://www.kulichki.com/tolkien/arhiv/manuscr/genezis.shtml>); there is a revised edition in *Recovery and Transcendence for the Contemporary*

Mythmaker. The Spiritual Dimension in the Works of J. R. R. Tolkien, Zurich and Berne: Walking Tree Publishers, Cormarë Series 7, 2004.

Garnier, Philippe, 2003, 'Eriol ou Ælfwine le marin' and 'Les traditions textuelles des Jours anciens. Les voies de transmission des légendes des "auteurs-acteurs" à l'"éditeur-auteur" moderne', in *La Feuille de la Compagnie*, No. 2 (Michaël Devaux, (ed.), *Tolkien, les racines du légendaire*), Geneva: Ad Solem, pp. 157-180 and 283-311.

Garth, John, 2003, *Tolkien and the Great War*, London: HarperCollins.

Giannone, Carla, 1984, '*Ainulindalë*: la cosmologia tradizionale di J. R. R. Tolkien', *Letterature*, Facoltà di magistro dell'Università di Genova. Istituto di lingue et letterature straniere, 7, pp. 168-179.

Giessl, Thomas, 2006, 'Ainulindalen', in *Hither Shore*, Band 3, pp. 151-164.

Harvey, David, 1985, *The Song of Middle-earth: J. R. R. Tolkien's Themes, Symbols and Myths*, London: Allen & Unwin.

Helms, Randel, 1981, *Tolkien and the Silmarils*, London: Thames and Hudson.

Houghton, John William, 2002, 'Augustine in the cottage of lost play. The *Ainulindalë* as asterisk cosmogony', in Jane Chance (ed.), *Tolkien the Medievalist*, London: Routledge.

Irigaray, Fr. Ricardo SJ, 1999, *Elfos, Hobbits y Dragones. Una investigaión sobre la simbología de Tolkien*, Buenos Aires: Tierra Media.

Kilby, C. S, 1977, *Tolkien and The Silmarillion*, Wheaton, IL: Harold Shaw.

Lacoste, Jean-Yves, 1984, 'Les anges musiciens. Considérations sur l'éternité, à partir de thèmes iconographiques et musicologiques', *Revue des sciences philosophiques et théologiques*, 68, 4, pp.549-575.

Lewis, C. S., 1964, *The Discarded Image*, Cambridge: CUP.

Murray, Fr. Robert SJ, 1998, 'J. R. R. Tolkien and the Art of the Parable', in Joseph Pearce (ed.), *Tolkien. A Celebration*, London: HarperCollins, pp. 40-52.

Noad, Charles E., 2000, 'On the construction of "The Silmarillion"', in Verlyn Flieger & Carl F. Hostetter (eds.), *Tolkien's* Legendarium. Essays on The History of Middle-Earth, Westport and London: Greenwood Press.

Pény, Jean-Marie, 1996, Chap. XVI in Jean Duchesne (ed.), *Histoire chrétienne de la littérature. L'Esprit des Lettres de l'Antiquité à nos jours*, Paris: Flammarion.

Pirson, Ron, 1998, 'The Elder Days. The Biblical Primeval History and *The Silmarillion*', in Sjoerd van der Weide (ed.), in *Proceedings of* Unquendor's *Third Lustrum Conference held in Delft, 25 May 1996*, Leiden, *Lembas-extra*, pp. 56-72.

Purtill, Richard, 2003, 'Tolkien's Creation Myth' (first published 1984), in *J. R. R. Tolkien. Myth, Morality, and Religion*, San Francisco: Ignatius Press.

Qadri, Jean-Philippe, 'La narration dans l'*Ainulindalë*', work in progress posted on <http://www.jrrvf.com/forum/noncgi/Forum1/HTML/001005.html> from 11th November 2003 on.

Schweicher, Eric, 1995, 'Aspects of the Fall in *The Silmarillion*', in Patricia Reynolds and Glen H. GoodKnight (eds.), *Proceedings of the J. R. R. Tolkien Centenary Conference*, Milton Keynes: The Tolkien Society / Altadena: The Mythopoeic Press, pp. 167-171.

Scull, Christina, 2000, 'The development of Tolkien's *legendarium*. Some Threads in the Tapestry of Middle-Earth', in Verlyn Flieger & Carl F. Hostetter (eds.), *Tolkien's* Legendarium. *Essays on* The History of Middle-Earth, Westport and London: Greenwood Press.

Shippey, Thomas A, 1992, *The Road to Middle-earth*, (2nd edition, first published 1982), London: HarperCollins.

Timmons, Daniel, 1998, 'Sub-creator and Creator: Tolkien and the Design of the One', in Agøy 1998a, pp. 52-68.

Tolkien, J. R. R., 1983, *The Book of Lost Tales, Part 1*, ed. Christopher Tolkien (= *The History of Middle-Earth*, Vol. I) London: George Allen and Unwin.

—, 1987, *The Lost Road*, ed. Christopher Tolkien (= *The History of Middle-Earth*, Vol. V), London: Unwin Hyman.

—, 1992, *Sauron Defeated*, ed. Christopher Tolkien (= *The History of Middle-Earth*, Vol. IX), London: HarperCollins.

—, 1993, *Morgoth's Ring*, ed. Christopher Tolkien (= *The History of Middle-Earth*, Vol. X), London: HarperCollins.

—, 1994, *The War of the Jewels*, ed. Christopher Tolkien (= *The History of Middle-Earth*, Vol. XI), London: HarperCollins.

—, 1998, 'The Qenya Lexicon', ed. by Christopher Gilson, Carl F. Hostetter, Patrick Wynne, and Arden R. Smith, in *Parma Eldalamberon* 12, 1998, pp. 29-106.

Vramming, Ylva, 1985, 'The Music of the Ainur – *Ainulindalë*. Undersökning av en myt i J. R. R. Tolkien *The Silmarillion*', Professor Tord Olssone forskarseminarium 12 April 1985, [Uppsala], 23 pp. [Typescript].

Whittingham, Elizabeth A., 1998, 'The Mythology of the *Ainulindalë*: Tolkien's Creation of Hope', in *Journal of the Fantastic in the Arts*, 9, 3, No. 35, pp. 212-228.

From Mythopoeia to Mythography: Tolkien, Lönnrot, and Jerome

JASON FISHER

Abstract

Much attention has been lavished on the chain of influences from Elias Lönnrot's *Kalevala* to J.R.R. Tolkien's *Legendarium*, and a smaller amount, but still some, has been paid to the connections between it and Jerome's *Biblia Vulgata* (Latin Vulgate Bible). But heretofore, very little mention has been made of the fact that Tolkien's son and literary executor, Christopher, played an equally important role in the selection, editing, organization – and in some cases, even elaboration – of the raw materials his father left behind into a purportedly cohesive and final work; or to the fact that this was analogous to the work done by Jerome and Lönnrot in their respective projects. In essence, without Christopher, we might have had a 'Silmarillion,' in the loosest sense of that term, but we would not have had *The Silmarillion*. Whether and to what degree Christopher's realization of his father's work is ultimately true to his father's wishes, however, is another matter, and one I will also touch on in this paper.

For a long time, my lays have been in the cold,   housed in darkness.
Shall I pull the lays out of the cold,   draw the songs out of the frost,
bring my box into the house   to the end of the long bench
under the fine ridgepole,   under the lovely roof?
Shall I open my chest of words,   unlock my song box [...?]

Kalevala, Runo 1

I am not getting on fast with The S[ilmarillion] [...] When you pray for me, pray for 'time'! I should like to put some of this stuff into readable form, and some sketched for others to make use of.

J.R.R. Tolkien (in a letter to his son, Michael, 1970)

J.R.R. Tolkien's *The Silmarillion*, posthumously realized by his son and literary executor, Christopher Tolkien, is often called "a difficult work" and is frequently likened in its structure, form, and language to another "difficult" work, the Bible. And indeed, the resemblance is much more than superficial. The Bible, like other similar collections of mythological and cosmogonic material, is essentially a constructed work, and one for which the final judgment as to the canonicity of its various components is still a matter of protracted debate. For example, one thinks of the contention between Jerome's *Biblia Vulgata* (more often referred to as the Latin Vulgate Bible), the *Vetus Latina*, the Septuagint, and the Jewish Tanakh. By his acts of selection and translation, Jerome produced what one might venture to call a "Silmarillion" for the Roman Catholic Church: the Latin Vulgate Bible, a work with which Tolkien would have been intimately familiar. By analogy, then, the bulk of Tolkien's unpublished writings – often internally inconsistent, frequently undated, and habitually emended – represent something like the mass of original religious writings which, over time, have coalesced into one canonical "book" or another. In the same way, Christopher Tolkien's edition of *The Silmarillion* represents one such attempt at consistency and canonicity; however, it is certainly not the only one possible.

And the Bible, too, represents only one such precedent. Elias Lönnrot, an acknowledged influence on and source for Tolkien, performed a task in his selection and preparation of the Finnish national epic, *The Kalevala*, which was quite comparable to that of Christopher Tolkien's collation and preparation of *The Silmarillion*. And he faced similar dilemmas. In her excellent essay, "Identifying England's Lönnrot", Anne Petty writes that

> [t]he problem of textualization applies as well to Christopher Tolkien's published form of the *Silmarillion*. Did his father intend the tales to be ordered in that way or for those versions to become the published ones? No one knew his father's mind better than Christopher regarding the state of the Silmarillion material, yet even so, [...] [l]ike Lönnrot, Christopher Tolkien was required to make executive decisions, some small (punctuation and spelling consistency) and some larger (arrangement and

sequencing), in order to publish a "master" version from many different versions and fragments available. (2004: 77).

In the end, Christopher Tolkien's work on the published *Silmarillion*, like that of the other great mythographers, Jerome and Elias Lönnrot (and others—e.g. Hesiod, Euhemerus, Snorri Sturluson, Jacob Grimm, Nikolaj Grundtvig, just to name a few of the best-known and most important to Tolkien studies), was an attempt to make sense out of his father's "body of more or less connected legend" (Tolkien 1981: 144); and for good or ill, the work now stands as something like a canonical text, despite the unavoidable intrusions of its editor. Indeed, the treatment of the published *Silmarillion* as canonical began with Christopher Tolkien himself, as he explains in his introduction to *Unfinished Tales*: "I have indeed treated the published form of *The Silmarillion* as a fixed point of reference of the same order as the writings published by my father himself, without taking into account the innumerable 'unauthorized' decisions between variants and rival versions that went into its making" (Tolkien 1980: 3). And since 1977, the majority of Tolkien scholars have done likewise.[1]

MYTHOPOEIA: THE *KALEVALA*, THE LATIN VULGATE BIBLE, AND *THE SILMARILLION*

Humphrey Carpenter dates Tolkien's first encounter with the *Kalevala* to around 1911, making him about nineteen years old. Tolkien first read the work in W.H. Kirby's English translation at King Edward's School in Birmingham, but he was so taken with the work that when he discovered Charles Eliot's *Finnish Grammar* in the Exeter College library, he "began an assault on the original language of the poems" (Carpenter 1977: 59) in an

---

[1] For an example, Randel Helms writes in *Tolkien and the Silmarils* that "[t]his [...] strikes me as a sensible way of treating *The Silmarillion*, and it is this way I have approached it in the present study – as a finished book surrounded by a nimbus of discarded or incomplete versions, some of which may have their own interest and published existence" (Helms 1981: 95).

effort to master enough of it that he might read the Finnish national epic in its native tongue. Tolkien's interest in the *Kalevala* remained unabated three years later when he wrote to his fiancée Edith Bratt that, "[a]mongst other work, I am trying to turn one of the stories – which is really a very great story and most tragic – into a short story somewhat on the lines of Morris' romances with chunks of poetry in between" (Tolkien 1981: 7). Some forty years later, Tolkien would go on to acknowledge the debt even more explicitly, writing to W.H. Auden:

> I mentioned Finnish, because that set the rocket off in story. I was immensely attracted by something in the air of the Kalevala, even in Kirby's poor translation. I never learned Finnish well enough to do more than plod through a bit of the original, like a schoolboy with Ovid; being mostly taken up with its effect on 'my language'. But the beginning of the legendarium, of which the Trilogy is part (the conclusion), was in an attempt to reorganize some of the Kalevala, especially the tale of Kullervo the hapless, into a form of my own.
> (Tolkien 1981: 214)

Tolkien's retelling of the story of Kullervo, alas, was never completed; however, traces of the influence of the *Kalevala* on his earliest creative attempts abound – for instance, in the poem "Narqelion", dating from somewhere between November 1915 and March 1916 (Carpenter 1977: 76). The poem, only partly (and poorly) transcribed in Carpenter's biography, has appeared several times subsequently, and various translations have been attempted.[2] One notes among its Finnish-influenced Q[u]enya[3] words the

---

[2] Carpenter provides only four of the poem's twenty lines, and he mistranscribes *kuluvai* as *kuluvi*. The poem was first printed in its entirety in *Mythlore* 56 (1988) with an analysis by Paul Nolan Hyde. Subsequently, the poem appeared in *Vinyar Tengwar* 6 (1989) and then again in *Vinyar Tengwar* 12 (1990), with a translation by Paul Nolan Hyde and a synopsis by Jorge Quiñones. Still later, the poem was reprinted with an accompanying article by Patrick Wynne and Christopher Gilson in *Parma Eldalemberon* 9 (1990). And finally, the poem, a translation and detailed analysis by Christopher Gilson (bolstered by new material made available with the publication of the Qenya Lexicon in *Parma*

conspicuous presence of the word *kuluvai*. One cannot help but observe the similarity between this word and the name, Kullervo. And though Carpenter records that no translation by Tolkien for the poem exists, the word, *kuluvai*, is clearly related to the Q[u]enya root √KUL "golden-red" (Tolkien 1987: 365).[4] Christopher Gilson, in fact, has determined that *kuluvai* is the plural of the adjective *kuluva* "of gold" (Gilson 1999: 20).[5] And the Finnish name, Kullervo, appears to have a cognate meaning; as Magoun points out, "the name, of disputed origin, is possibly based on *kulta* (gen. *kullan*) 'gold, dear one'" (1963: 395). Clearly, this is just the sort of detail Tolkien would have unearthed, and thus it seems evident that *kuluvai* in the poem is a deliberate echo of Kullervo, in both sound and sense.

The impact of the *Kalevala* may also be felt in the earliest *Lost Tales*, on which Tolkien began work around 1915. Without belaboring the point, I'd like to offer just one example. One of the first tales at which Tolkien tried his hand (around the same time he wrote to Edith that he was tinkering with the Kullervo story) was *The Cottage of Lost Play*, discussed at length by Christopher Tolkien in *The Book of Lost Tales, Part One*. In April, 1915, Tolkien wrote the first draft of a poem to accompany the tale – perhaps meant as one of the "chunks of poetry in between." The poem, called "You & Me and the Cottage of Lost Play", begins with these lines:

> You and me – we know that land
> And often have been there
> In the long old days, old nursery days,
> A dark child and a fair.

Eldalamberon 12), and a facsimile of Tolkien's original manuscript appeared in *Vinyar Tengwar* 40 (1999).

[3] Throughout this chapter, I have used the form "Q[u]enya" so as to avoid a lengthy and digressive explanation of the distinction between the very early form of the language, called Qenya, and the later, more mature form, called Quenya. Such a distinction is unnecessary to the overall thread of my arguments here.

[4] In fact, the gloss of "golden-red" for this root is an emendation; the earlier original meaning was "gold (metal)."

[5] The word *kuluva* "of gold", and its related root √KULU are given in the Qenya Lexicon (Tolkien 1998: 49).

> [...]
> That You and I got lost in Sleep
> > And met each other there –
> Your dark hair on your white nightgown,
> > And mine was tangled fair.
> (Tolkien 1984a: 28)

Here, rather than a deeply embedded linguistic allusion, it appears that we are hearing an echo[6] of the opening of the *Kalevala*, together with a rough approximation of its style. Compare the preceding lines with this portion of Runo 1 from the *Kalevala*:

> Beloved friend, my boon companion,   my fair boyhood comrade,
> start now to sing with me,   begin to recite together
> now that we have come together,   have come from two directions.
> Seldom do we come together,   meet one another
> on these wretched marches,   these poor northern parts.
> Let us clasp hand in hand,   fingers in fingers,
> so that we may sing fine things [...]
> (Magoun 1963: 3)

The similarities seem more than coincidental (except that, where in the *Kalevala* we have "seldom," Tolkien has reversed the meaning to "often"). Also, take note of the use of repetition in the third line of the Tolkien poem – "long old days, old nursery days" – where we see precisely the sort of stylistic repetition for which the *Kalevala* is so well known (Magoun 1963: xix-xx).

It is clear, then, that the *Kalevala* had a very profound impact on Tolkien's early story-making – in his own words, as he wrote to Auden, it "set the rocket off." And its potent influence would be felt not just in Tolkien's experimental juvenilia, more often abandoned than finished, but throughout his entire *legendarium*, at which he labored constantly during the course of his entire adult life. As he admitted to his son Christopher in 1944,

---

[6] Appropriately, this is almost literally an echo, in the sense of the echoing, repetitious style of both poems.

"Finnish nearly ruined my Hon. Mods, and was the original germ of the Silmarillion" (Tolkien 1981: 87), a sentiment he echoed again in a 1964 letter to Christopher Bretherton: "The germ of my attempt to write legends of my own to fit my private languages was the tragic tale of the hapless Kullervo in the Finnish *Kalevala*. It remains a major matter in the legends of the First Age (which I hope to publish as *The Silmarillion*)" (Tolkien 1981: 345).

By way of a brief digression, it is worth pointing out that the *Kalevala* also affected Tolkien's artwork and his visual conception of aspects of his *legendarium*. A key example of this may be found in Tolkien's watercolor, "The Land of Pohja,"[7] painted in December, 1914. The subject of Tolkien's painting goes directly to a vignette in the *Kalevala* involving the wizard, Väinämöinen, and it represents "another precursor of the 'Silmarillion' mythology, for the *Kalevala* episode of the theft of the Sun and Moon almost certainly influenced Tolkien's pivotal tale of the destruction of the Two Trees, the theft of the Silmarils, and the Darkening of Valinor" (Hammond and Scull 1995: 44-5).

And of course, Tolkien's immersion in Finnish had an immeasurable effect on the development on his invented language, Q[u]enya. Rather than an Elven-Latin[8], Q[u]enya might just as aptly be called an Elven-Finnish. In addition to the possible relationship between Kullervo and *kuluvai*, previously mentioned, there are many other points of contact between the

---

[7] Today, Pohja is known as a municipality in the region of Uusimaa in southern Finland; however, in the context of the *Kalevala*, Pohja (and more often, Pohjola, which loosely means "Northland", deriving from Finnish *pohjoinen* "north" < *pohja* "bottom, foundation") is a region of extreme cold along the northern Lappish coasts and governed by the sorceress, Louhi. The struggle between the regions of Pohja and Kalevala forms the backdrop for the tragic tale of Kullervo. In Magoun, Pohja is rendered as "North Farm" (1963: 398). As a side note, the Q[u]enya word *pōya* "northern" seems to have been arisen from the Finnish Pohja.

[8] Tolkien referred to Q[u]enya in this way more than once; for example, see Tolkien 2004:1128, Tolkien 1981:176, and Tolkien 1992:241 (and passim), and while there is (or *was*, in its earlier stages) certainly a connection between the structure of Q[u]enya and that of Latin, I believe he came to mean the comparison more metaphorically than literally, referring to the significance of Latin as a liturgical and literary language in the historical context of our Primary World. The role of Q[u]enya, in his fictive Secondary World, was an analogous one.

languages. Again, for the sake of brevity, I'll give just a few examples here. First and most obviously, the phonology of Q[u]enya is very similar to Finnish, which influenced Tolkien though its "'phonaesthetic' pleasure" (Tolkien 1981: 176).[9] Second, many Finnish words have found close echoes in Q[u]enya. For instance, Aino, Joukahainen's sister in the *Kalevala*, takes her name from the Finnish adjective, *aino* "peerless, splendid" (Magoun 1963: 387), which may well have informed Tolkien's conception of the Ainur, the archangels of Arda. Another character from the *Kalevala*, Lemminkäinen, seems to have given his name to the Q[u]enya word, *leminkainen* "twenty-three" (Tolkien 1998: 52).[10] And then there is the obvious influence of the Finnish noun *ilma* "air, sky." In the *Kalevala*, the component appears in Ilmatar, the Air Spirit; and in Ilmarinen, the great smith who forges the Sampo, and whose name is generally taken to signify "maker of (the vault of) the sky" (Magoun 1963: 385, 392). In Tolkien's use, *ilma* occurs as the Q[u]enya noun for "Starlight", clearly related to the Finnish word; and Ilmarin ("mansion of the high airs") is the palace of Manwë and Varda atop Taniquetil (Tolkien 1977: 336, 360). There are many other examples as well – for instance, Untamo may have influenced Tolkien's Utumno, and *lohi-käärme* "flying serpent, dragon" (from Loviatar in the *Kalevala*, with a further echo of the Old Norse Loki) finds

---

[9] Tolkien also wrote elsewhere of "the acute aesthetic pleasure derived from a language for its own sake, not only free from being useful but free even from being the 'vehicle of a literature'" (Tolkien 1981: 213).

[10] Christopher Tolkien has speculated that Tolkien included the otherwise arbitrary number, "twenty-three", in his first Q[u]enya glosses because it represented his age at the time (Tolkien 1984a: 246). But however likely this may be, it is probably not the sole explanation, as Tolkien's word for "ten", *lempe*, is also very close to Lempi, the name of Lemminkäinen's father (and the two Finnish names, moreover, are linguistically related to one another). It may be going too far to wonder whether Tolkien felt any sense of personal identification with the character of Lemminkäinen, but clearly, the *Kalevala* seems to have been on his mind as he created number-words for his burgeoning language. however, it might be possible to set passages from the published *Silmarillion* side by side with the corresponding drafts published in *The History of Middle-earth* (or with the original manuscripts in the Bodleian, where necessary) and to systematically ascertain the precise nature and degree of alteration made by Christopher Tolkien and Guy Kay.

etymological resonance in Tolkien's Urulóki "fire serpent, dragon" (Tolkien 1977: 253) and Foalókë "treasure-guarding serpent" (Tolkien 1984b: 340).

I'd like to make one other observation on the influence of the Finnish language in Tolkien's formative years, in what might seem the unlikeliest of places: *The Father Christmas Letters*. Elaborating on the "back-story" of Father Christmas, Tolkien added an Elf, Ilbereth (a form which would eventually become Elbereth, a by-name for the Vala Varda), as well the North Polar Bear and the Polar Cubs, his two young nephews (Tolkien 1995: 5). The bears' names, it transpires, are all Finnish in form. The North Polar Bear's name, Karhu, is simply the Finnish word for "bear." Tolkien glosses his nephews' names, Paksu and Valkotukka as "fat" and "white-hair" (Tolkien 1995: 66). Digging a little deeper, *paksu* is indeed Finnish for "corpulent, fat, thick," but it seems to me that we may also find an echo of *pakkanen* "severe cold, bitterly freezing weather," a perfectly appropriate side-connotation for a North Polar Cub. And as for Valkotukka, Tolkien's calque may be explained as *valkea* "blank, white" + *takki* "cloak, mantle."

Having already hinted at one or two specific corollaries to the *Kalevala* in the "Silmarillion", I'd like to turn next to an overview of the common threads between J.R.R. Tolkien's larger "Silmarillion" mythology and the *Kalevala*. In the section to follow, I will be considering Christopher Tolkien's published *Silmarillion* (as differentiated from the loose and unfinished "Silmarillion" of his father) in the same context. Of course, any examination of shared elements and influences in two such closely connected works as the "Silmarillion" and the *Kalevala* in a short chapter such as this one must necessarily be rather perfunctory. Sufficient points of congruence exist to fill many articles, even entire books, and interested readers are referred to the bibliography at the conclusion of the chapter for studies of more depth on this particular subject.[11]

The Kullervo story (Runos 31-36), quite apart from Tolkien's early attempts to recast it as a short story, eventually fed the tale of the Children of

---

[11] For example, see Flieger, Gay, and West.

Húrin and the tragic fate of Túrin Turambar.[12] As Tom Shippey summarizes it so well:

> In both a hero survives the ruin of his family to grow up with a cruel, wayward streak in fosterage; in both he marries (or seduces) a lost maiden, only for her to discover she is his sister and drown herself; in both the hero returns from his exploits to find his mother gone and home laid waste, and to be condemned by his own associates.
> (Shippey 2003: 261)

Another major feature of the *Kalevala* to find an apparent home in *The Silmarillion* is the mysterious Sampo (scattered throughout the *Kalevala* in Runos 10, 38-9, 42-3, *inter alia*). In Tolkien's *legendarium*, the Sampo, at least in part, evolved into the Three Silmarils – which give their name to *The Silmarillion* as a whole. Jonathan Himes has written at length on exactly how Tolkien adapted the concept of this enigmatic mythological artifact for his own use, and I will simply refer readers to his excellent analysis rather than recapitulate it here. For my purposes, it suffices to say that:

> the *Sampo* may well be Tolkien's most remarkable borrowing. In *The Kalevala*, the *Sampo* is a strange and vaguely mythological object of power, over which the poles of good and evil struggle for control. But the inherent ambiguities of the *Sampo* permitted Tolkien to adapt it in whatever ways he wished – indeed, his choices may reveal something of his own personal ideas about the nature of the *Sampo*.
> (Fisher 2006: 613)

---

[12] As most readers will know, Christopher Tolkien has now published a complete edition of *The Children of Húrin* (April, 2007) in which – as he did with the published *Silmarillion* – he has omitted all scholarly intrusion and woven together the extant texts into a single, cohesive narrative. This publication marks the thirtieth anniversary of *The Silmarillion* with special significance.

One more commonality between the *Kalevala* and the Silmarillion is the use of song contests, songs of power, and enchantments. The most important example in the *Kalevala* is the "contest in magic singing" (Magoun 1963: 18) between the wizard, Väinämöinen, and the young upstart, Joukahainen, as recounted in Runo 3. This encounter finds a direct parallel in *The Silmarillion*, in "the contest of Sauron and Felagund which is renowned. For Felagund strove with Sauron in songs of power, and the power of the King was very great; but Sauron had the mastery, as is told in the Lay of Leithian" (Tolkien 1977: 170-1).[13]

In addition to these larger borrowings – the Sampo, the tale of Kullervo, and the contests of songs of power – I'd like to close with one or two additional comments on echoes of the Sampo in Tolkien's *legendarium*. For one, the lid of the Sampo is described as "of many colors" (see throughout Runo 10, Magoun 1963: 58, passim). This, it strikes me, is more than coincidentally similar to Saruman's self-imposed epithet, "Saruman of Many Colours" (Tolkien 2004: 259). Certainly Saruman's many-hued cloak may owe a larger debt to Joseph's coat of many colors from the Bible; however, it seems likely to me that the repetition of this precise phrase in the *Kalevala* may have stuck in Tolkien's ear, so to speak. And then there is "*Kampo* the Leaper, a name for Eärendel [sic]" (Garth 2003: 63).[14] Can it be mere chance that the name, Kampo, for a man associated with one of the Silmarils (or perhaps the word referred to the Star of Eärendil), should be so similar to Sampo, a key folkloric inspiration for the Silmarils? It may be no more than idle speculation, but I think not.

While the *Kalevala* certainly has much in common with *The Silmarillion*, the majority of these points of contact fall into the realm of content (that is, the suggestiveness of the stories related in the *Kalevala* on their counterparts in Tolkien) and language (that is, the influence of the

---

[13] The precedent of the magic and power of song in the *Kalevala* also informs the character of Tom Bombadil in *The Lord of the Rings*. (See Gay 2004)

[14] For the root of this rare name, √KAP "leap", see Tolkien 1987:362.

Finnish language on the phonology and morphology of Tolkien's Elvish language, Q[u]enya). But in terms of its *style*, *The Silmarillion* is not really very much like it at all. While the *Kalevala* consists entirely of poetry, *The Silmarillion* contains next to none – unlike *The Hobbit* and *The Lord of the Rings*, which are literally brimming over with verse. Once again, however, it should be acknowledged that this needn't have been the case; rather, this represents an example of the deliberate choices of its editor, Christopher Tolkien. *The Silmarillion* might well have been *full* of poetry, as many of the underlying tales and legends, many of which were later published in *The History of Middle-earth*, were composed in verse. For one example, Christopher elected not to include in *The Silmarillion* any of the thousands of lines of poetry that would later comprise the *Lays of Beleriand*. Clyde Kilby, who worked with Tolkien on the "Silmarillion" material during the summer of 1966, went so far as to claim that "Some of the manuscript of *The Silmarillion* is in verse form" (Kilby 1977: 32).

"All that 'heigh stile' (as Chaucer might say)" (Tolkien 1981: 238)[15] of the prose form of the published *Silmarillion* has, since the book debuted thirty years ago, reminded readers much more of the Bible than of anything else. Again and again, it has been compared to the Bible and its style labeled as "Biblical". In his review of *The Silmarillion* for the *New York Times*, for example, the novelist, John Gardner, a man who knew a thing or two about mythology himself, wrote:

> Strange man! Strange mind! Why would anyone do it, we keep asking as we read. Why create a whole Christianlike religion, a whole new creation myth to set beside those of the Greeks, the Jews, the Northmen and the rest? Why write a mythic history, a Bible?

---

[15] Tolkien used the same phrase (with a more modern spelling) several years earlier as well; see Tolkien 1981: 136.

In another very early response to *The Silmarillion*, Richard Matthews calls it "a difficult body of material" (1978:56)[16] and points out that "[t]he tale *begins* at the *beginning*, more like the *Bible* than like the classical epic, *in medias res*. It begins with Genesis [...]" (58).

These same opinions would come to be echoed again and again. Randel Helms calls *The Silmarillion* "Tolkien's most complex and challenging work" (1981: ix) and goes on to observe that "*Ainulindalë*, and indeed all *The Silmarillion*, finds a major source for its themes and structures in the Bible" (25). So, too, Paul Kocher notes that "[l]ike the Christian Book of Genesis *The Silmarillion* has, of course, only one God" (1980: 4). Jared Lobdell refers to "a 'Biblical' pastiche" (1981: 101), Richard Purtill comments that "the [primary] belief creates the myth, not the myth the belief" (1984: 7) and calls attention to "the basically religious character of Tolkien's thought ... much clearer in *The Silmarillion* than in the works published earlier" (119). Tom Shippey points out the congruence between "the Fall of Man and the Exile from the Garden of Eden in the *Book of Genesis* [and] the loss of elvish innocence and the emigration from Aman (which becomes an exile) in *The Silmarillion*" (Shippey 2000: 239). Even Christopher Tolkien reports that the character and style of the work led at least one reader to complain to him that "[i]t's like *the Old Testament!*" (Tolkien 1984a: 2). Indeed, one could cite example after example of the comparison.

But is the comparison to the Bible genuinely apt, or is it merely a misapplication of style or a misunderstanding on the part of critics? In this case, it is no misapplication or misunderstanding; there is ample evidence to call the comparison a legitimate one. And the points of contact between the Bible and *The Silmarillion*, we will see, extend beyond the purely stylistic and into the domain of content and theological influence as well. Indeed, I

---

[16] Christopher Tolkien himself echoes this assessment in the foreword to *The Book of Lost Tales, Part One*: "*The Silmarillion* is commonly said to be a 'difficult' book, needing explanation and guidance on how to 'approach' it" (Tolkien 1984a: 1).

think it's possible to argue that *The Lord of the Rings* has a distinctive flavor of the New Testament, while *The Silmarillion* is more colored by the Old.

It is "The Bible" as a generic artifact to which *The Silmarillion* is generally compared; however, we would do well to remember Tolkien's devout Roman Catholicism, the consequences of which are that a particular *variety* of Christianity with particular scriptural preferences is to be expected. He writes of his theological beliefs many times, and he famously declared that "*The Lord of the Rings* is of course a fundamentally religious and Catholic work; unconsciously so at first, but consciously in the revision" (Tolkien 1981: 172). Of course, if this is true of *The Lord of the Rings*, we have every reason to suspect it's true of *The Silmarillion*, a work he spent considerably more time developing, ruminating on, and revising. And we have more than mere supposition. Carpenter provides a convincing reply to Gardner's rhetorical question – "Why would anyone do it[?]" – when he writes:

> Some have puzzled over the relation between Tolkien's stories and his Christianity, and have found it difficult to understand how a devout Roman Catholic could write with such conviction about a world where God is not worshipped. But there is no mystery. *The Silmarillion* is the work of a profoundly religious man. It does not contradict Christianity but complements it. There is in the legends no worship of God, yet God is indeed there, *more explicitly in The Silmarillion than in the work that grew out of it, The Lord of the Rings*.
> (Carpenter 1977: 91, emphasis mine)

And as a Catholic influence, not all Bibles are created equal; the Latin Vulgate Bible would have been the most likely template for Tolkien's Catholic (re)vision, as it is still the principal text used by Roman Catholics today. We can therefore be certain that Tolkien would have known it well and may also have been familiar with other works of its compiler and translator, Jerome – the man who would later be canonized as a Catholic saint. Jerome's work would also have interested Tolkien on a philological level. Around the year 390, Jerome undertook the enormous (and, in his own day, largely thankless) task of executing an entirely fresh translation of the Bible from what were then believed to be the earliest extant texts in their original languages (Hebrew, Aramaic, and Greek). Scholars have since learned that some of these texts did not, in fact, preserve the oldest readings of the scripture – in years after, not unlike discovering a Tolkien draft that antedates all other known versions, Biblical scholarship has revealed that Jerome was not always on the correct page, so to speak. Yet he was, of course, unaware of this at the time and set about his work in good faith (Kelly 1998: 159-67).

Jerome carried out his new translation because he was unhappy with the older Latin translation, the collection of texts referred to as the *Vetus Latina*. There was also considerable debate between Christians and Jews on the theological issues of the day, and much of the debate centered on the Jewish community's questioning of the validity and accuracy of the contemporary Latin Bible. Jerome's efforts, therefore, were largely aimed at mitigating such questions by producing a new translation from the original sources. This desire to return to the source, as it were, would have appealed to Tolkien, and indeed, Tolkien himself contributed to the new translation into English known as the Jerusalem Bible, translating Jonah, just as Jerome himself had done centuries earlier.[17]

Throughout *The Silmarillion* (as in *The Lord of the Rings*), one finds echoes of the Latin Vulgate. As I mentioned earlier, the majority of the Biblical parallels in *The Silmarillion* are of the Old Testament variety (while those of *The Lord of the Rings* tend to come from the Gospels). The most

---

[17] Tolkien translated Jonah – not directly from the Hebrew as is so often supposed, but from the French (Scull and Hammond 2006: 438, Kilby 1977: 54), though he did pursue some study Hebrew at one point during 1957 (Scull and Hammond 2006: 468) – and "consulted on one or two points of style" (Tolkien 1981: 378). In addition, one of Jerome's earlier works was an *Onomasticon* of the etymologies of Hebrew personal and place names (see Kelly 1998: 153-54). This would no doubt have held much interest for Tolkien (if he knew of it), and one might easily compare it to Tolkien's own Q[u]enya lexicons as well as the "Nomenclature" he prepared for translators of *The Lord of the Rings* (Hammond and Scull 2005: 750-82).

obvious example, naturally, is in Tolkien's Creation Story, the *Ainulindalë*, which closely echoes parts of the Book of Genesis – and to which I've already alluded. But there are also numerous echoes of Exodus (by way of the *Old English Exodus*, of which Tolkien produced an edition), Ezekiel (Helms 1981: 28), Samuel (Helms 1981: 40), Job (Helms 1981: 27), Numbers (Isaacs 2004: 6), and the Psalms (Shippey 2003: 200). No doubt many other examples might be found.

MYTHOGRAPHY: ELIAS LÖNNROT, SAINT JEROME, AND CHRISTOPHER TOLKIEN

It should be very clear by this point that the *Kalevala* and the Latin Vulgate Bible had a profound impact of Tolkien's fictive world-making, starting at an early formative stage and extending throughout his long life. But what of the final assembly of this work by his son and literary executor, Christopher Tolkien, into the single unified narrative of *The Silmarillion*, as published after his father's death?[18] What is most ironic about this undertaking is that, in collecting together, organizing, editing, and in some cases even (re)writing portions of the narrative, Christopher took on a role analogous to that adopted by Elias Lönnrot in Finland during the middle of the 19th century and by Jerome at the end of the fourth century. But whereas, for Lönnrot, the raw materials consisted of the songs and poems of the rural Finnish rune-singers and, for Jerome, they were comprised of an extant (if debatable) scriptural canon, for Christopher, the raw materials consisted of the enormous masses of unpublished and unordered notes, drafts, poems, and tales left behind in the wake of his father's passing.[19] Or, to put it another way, where J.R.R. Tolkien may have been emulating the *product* of

---

[18] Not to mention *Unfinished Tales* and *The Children of Húrin*.

[19] The German scholar Friedhelm Schneidewind refers to the materials collected in *The History of Middle-earth* as a *Zettelkasten* – a "box of slips (or, a pile of notes)" (private correspondence), which seems a particularly apt description to me.

Lönnrot's and Jerome's efforts, Christopher Tolkien was emulating the process.[20]

Throughout his professional life, Lönnrot would be haunted by the struggle for completeness, just as both Tolkien and his son, Christopher, would be a century later. He wrote in his foreword to *A Collection of Songs about Väinämöinen* (published posthumously in 1892):[21]

> The following collection of songs about Väinämöinen is presented not with the idea or hope that it is in any way complete but with the thought and hope through this of better filling out what is lacking. Of course it is easier to improve a road once it has been constructed than to construct a new one from nothing, and from this collection everybody can now better see what has already been collected [...] and what is now lacking.
> (quoted in Magoun 1963: 363)

This very description, *mutatis mutandis*, could apply equally well to Christopher Tolkien's work on the published *Silmarillion*. He writes that "[a] complete consistency (either within the compass of *The Silmarillion* itself or between *The Silmarillion* and other published writings of my father's) is not to be looked for, and could only be achieved, if at all, at heavy and needless cost" (Tolkien 1977: 8). Later, in Lönnrot's preface to the so-called *Old Kalevala* (i.e., the first edition), he wrote, again, that "[e]ven after these songs have finally been got ready for publication, they are indeed still woefully incomplete" (Magoun 365). And still later, in his preface to the so-called *New Kalevala* (i.e., the second edition), published in 1849, Lönnrot

---

[20] One can argue that J.R.R. Tolkien, to some extent, also emulated the process – as Verlyn Flieger notes, "I propose that Tolkien envisioned himself doing exactly that [...]. But with this difference – [...] He was a writer, not a collector. He would invent, and by connecting his invented myths to England's extant history he would interweave a whole tapestry where only disconnected scraps of information had been before" (Flieger 2004: 281) – however, with his death, he left us just the scraps, and in my view, it was clearly Christopher, much more so than his father, who actually followed Lönnrot's working example as a dedicated collector and organizer.

[21] The fact that some of Lönnrot's earliest work lay unpublished and only loosely organized until after his death nicely prefigures the same situation in Tolkien's life a century later.

explained that "[t]he present book [...] now appears in a much fuller form than what was in its previous state, and will very likely remain in its present form; for relevant uncollected songs of this type can no longer be found ..." (Magoun 374).

Indeed the series of choices facing Christopher Tolkien in the wake of his father's death must have seemed rather like a devil's bargain. He alludes to the particular challenges in his introduction to *Unfinished Tales*:

> The problems that confront one given responsibility for the writings of a dead author are hard to resolve. Some persons in this position may elect to make no material whatsoever available for publication, save perhaps for work that was in a virtually finished state at the time of the author's death. In the case of the unpublished writings of J.R.R. Tolkien this might seem at first sight the proper course; since he himself, peculiarly critical and exacting of his own work, would not have dreamt of allowing even the more completed narratives in this book to appear without much further refinement.
> On the other hand, the nature and scope of his invention seems to me to place even his abandoned stories in a peculiar position.
> (Tolkien 1980: 1)

To put this another way: the choice was between making nothing unfinished available posthumously; making everything available, no matter how unclear, disordered, or inconsistent; or attempting to strike a balance between these two extremes. Christopher goes on to assert: "[t]hat *The Silmarillion* should remain unknown was for me out of the question, despite its disordered state, and despite my father's known if very largely unfulfilled intentions for its transformation; and in that case I presumed, after long hesitation, to present the work not in the form of an historical study, a complex of divergent texts interlinked by commentary, but as a completed and cohesive entity" (1).

This is much the same approach Lönnrot elected for the *Kalevala*; rather than present it as a scholarly study, filled with abstruse cross-references and voluminous footnotes and other editorial apparatus, he organized and arranged the entire collection of poems into a single unified whole. Of course, this choice comes with its own array of consequences. The work is, for all its effectiveness in stirring up Finnish national pride, still "essentially a conflation and concatenation of a considerable number and variety of traditional songs, narrative, lyric, and magic," which "[o]wing to the special character of its compilation or concatenation [...] possesses no particular unity of style" (Magoun 1963: xiii, xiv). This, of course, finds great congruence in Tolkien, as Christopher writes: "Moreover, my father came to conceive *The Silmarillion* as a compilation, a compendious narrative, made long afterwards from sources of great diversity (poems, and annals, and oral tales) that had survived in agelong tradition; and this conception has indeed its parallel in the actual history of the book, for a great deal of earlier prose and poetry does underlie it, and it is to some extent a compendium in fact and not only in theory" (Tolkien 1977: 8).

This would have made for a challenging enough text all on its own, but the problems facing Christopher were exacerbated by the fact that *The Silmarillion*

> was far indeed from being a fixed text, and did not remain unchanged even in certain fundamental ideas concerning the nature of the world it portrays; while the same legends came to be retold in longer and shorter forms, and in different styles. As the years passed the changes and variants, both in detail and in larger perspectives, became so complex, so pervasive, and so many-layered that a final and definitive version seemed unattainable.
> (Tolkien 1977: 7)

Yet Christopher elected to undertake the challenge of bringing the "Silmarillion" papers into some kind of cohesive order, and the published

Silmarillion was the result. Yet again, it is important to realize that Christopher's solution to the problem is not the only possible one.

If Tolkien did indeed conceive of the "Silmarillion" tradition as a collection or collation of different texts, poems, annals, and so forth, it may be that he was deliberately attempting to create an illusion of historically conditioned diversity. But if so, then Christopher as his editor had to confront the choice of whether or how far to reflect that diversity in the published work. In the event, Christopher took a minimalist view, as contrasted with a maximalist view such as Charles Noad's.[22] The subsequent publication of *The History of Middle-earth*, moreover, might be seen as the maximalist counterpoint to the minimalist *Silmarillion* of 1977. At the same time, Christopher would have been faced with the challenge of gaining some measure of literary acceptance for the work his father had failed to complete, and a maximalist approach might have run counter to this goal. Certainly the choice cannot have been an easy one, and Christopher himself has acknowledged his missteps at various points in the years since its publication.[23]

Returning to the *Kalevala*, Anne Petty underscores the similarities between Lönnrot and Christopher Tolkien very well when she writes:

> In an ironic case of life imitating art imitating life, Christopher Tolkien, as literary executor, performed for his father's repository of invented mythology and legends the same kind of service Lönnrot accomplished for the Finnish folk epic. Looked at from this perspective, the label of "England's Lönnrot" applies equally well to both father and son, although for very different reasons. (2004: 70).

Petty's article is concerned much more with the father than the son; however, for my purposes, it is Christopher's work at collecting, organizing,

---

[22] See Noad's "On the Construction of 'The Silmarillion'".
[23] For instance, see Tolkien 1994:140, 356.

collating, editing, and even embellishing his father's scattered writings that is most at issue.

One point which is often overlooked in discussions of *The Silmarillion* – either intentionally or as a consequence of Christopher Tolkien's modesty – is the fact that Christopher was required in some cases to take a more active hand in the narrative. In particular, some of the final tales in the *Quenta Silmarillion* had been so long abandoned by his father that they were strikingly inconsistent with much of the rest of *The Silmarillion*. These sections, with input and assistance from Guy Kay, who worked with Christopher Tolkien in 1974-75, had to be rewritten, at least in part, to bring them into harmony with the rest of the work. Perhaps the best example of this kind of alteration of the original material lies in the "Ruin of Doriath", itself a rather ruinous collection of drafts that had become largely incompatible with the larger *Quenta Silmarillion*. Of this, Christopher wrote:

> Guy Kay took a major part, and *the chapter that I finally wrote* owes much to my discussions with him. It is, and was, obvious that a step was being taken of a different order from any other 'manipulation' of my father's own writing in the course of the book [...] [T]here was here an inescapable choice: either to abandon that [Tolkien's disharmonious] conception, or else to alter the story. I think now that this was a mistaken view, and that the undoubted difficulties could have been, and should have been, surmounted without so far overstepping the bounds of the editorial function.
> (Tolkien 1994: 356, emphasis mine)

The full extent of these changes, both in the "Ruin of Doriath" and elsewhere, is not immediately clear – this is one of the side-effects of an invisible editorial hand – however, it might be possible to set passages from the published *Silmarillion* side by side with the corresponding drafts published in *The History of Middle-earth* (or with the original manuscripts in the Bodleian, where necessary) and to systematically ascertain the precise nature and degree of alteration made by Christopher Tolkien and Guy Kay. To undertake that analysis is outside the scope of my paper, and the particulars are not central to my argument in any case. What is important to realize is that Christopher became, perforce, much more than mere editor in certain sections of *The Silmarillion*. And Lönnrot, it might be noted, acted similarly in the *Kalevala*, writing his own introductory and concluding verses to bookend those he had spent years collecting and organizing.[24]

Elias Lönnrot was not Christopher's only model for the assembly of *The Silmarillion*. Jerome faced many similar kinds of problems more than a thousand years before. Although, today, we normally think of the Bible as a fairly well established canon of books in a set sequence, this tradition was much less fixed in Jerome's day – although it was never so *unfixed* as the mass of Tolkien's unpublished writings had been. One of the most significant decisions that confronted Jerome was the question of whether or not to include the so-called deuterocanonical[25] books. These ten or so additional books (and parts of books), often loosely and pejoratively equated with the Apocrypha, are generally excluded from Protestant Bibles; however, thanks in part to Jerome's work, they are an important component of the Vulgate and, therefore, an essential element of Roman Catholicism today.

Perhaps ironically, Jerome initially hesitated on the inclusion of the deuterocanonical texts in the scope of his project. Without descending into a lengthy and arcane digression on the history of these texts, let it suffice to

---

[24] The specific verses in question are ll.1-110 of Runo 1 and ll.513-620 of Runo 50, which Magoun dismisses as "artless ... pure flights of Lönnrot's fantasy" (xv). These, to my mind, are clearly analogous to Christopher Tolkien's and Guy Kay's creative intrusions (necessary though they may have been); however, I would hesitate to dismiss them as quickly as Magoun does Lönnrot's. For additional information on Lönnrot's original verses, refer to Shippey 2003: 349-50.

[25] The term "deuterocanonical" derives from the Greek and means "belonging to the second canon." These books are so described because they come primarily from the Greek Septuagint, rather than from the primary (or "protocanonical") books of the Hebrew Bible. The term does not, as is often mistakenly supposed at first glance, have anything to do with the Old Testament Book of Deuteronomy.

say that the contention between the Alexandrian canon (represented by the Greek Septuagint) and the Hebraic canon after the first century led to much uncertainty as to the status of the deuterocanonical books. Jerome would have initially accepted them as part of the Septuagint, then rejected them when he moved to embrace the "Hebraica veritas", then finally adopted a kind of tense acceptance of them as *scriptural*, but not *canonical*. In the event, he translated and included them with the admonition that they be used "for edifying the people, not for the corroboration of ecclesiastical truths" (quoted in Kelly 1998: 160-1).

In the end, and despite much debate among the scholars of the day (notably between Jerome and Augustine), the Vulgate evolved into the canonical text for the Roman Catholic church. But just as *The Silmarillion* represents only one possible arrangement of Tolkien's source material, including some texts and excluding others, so too Jerome's Vulgate represents only one of many possible "Bibles". In this case, it happens to be the one Tolkien, both the father and the son, would have known and revered. The textual histories of both *The Silmarillion* and the Latin Vulgate are tangled and complex, and in both cases a later editor had much influence on the form that each work would finally take.

CONCLUDING REMARKS

The truth of the matter is that what we are celebrating in the thirtieth anniversary of the publication of *The Silmarillion* must be regarded as a collaborative effort between J.R.R. Tolkien and his third son. As Anne Petty aptly puts it: "the material comprising Tolkien's legendarium [...] would, in fact, prove to be greater than one person could master, eventually pulling son Christopher into its shaping as well" (2004: 82).[26] Doubtless, the task could have been approached from any number of angles, and the resulting

---

[26] Even before Tolkien's death, work on the "Silmarillion" had drawn in Clyde Kilby, who provided "the assistance of a scholar at once sympathetic and yet critical" (Kilby 1977: 17, Tolkien 1981: 366), "editorial and critical assistance" (Kilby 1977: 18). Even more than this, "Tolkien needed someone not so much to give him literary criticism as to press him, one way or another, into renewed attention to it" (Kilby 1977: 44).

Silmarillion would have differed – probably markedly – according to the approached taken.

Regardless of the path Christopher *did* take and irrespective of all those paths he might have taken but did not, Rayner Unwin is right to remind us that "[w]e owe Christopher an enormous debt for letting us share the totality of his father's work and understand, at least a little, the manner of its composition" (Unwin 2000: 4). We have understood much more of that manner of composition since the publication of *The History of Middle-earth*. And moreover, whether we agree with some, all, or none of Christopher's editorial choices, we must concur that

> the complexity of the material, its ever-expanding ramifications, and a reluctance to finalise any part for fear of destabilising some other aspect, made the completion of "The Silmarillion" impossible during his father's lifetime.

Its construction, as Unwin also points out, was an "unobtrusive task of great skill for that has never been adequately recognised", and we would do well to remember this the next time we open the time-worn pages of *The Silmarillion*. At the same time, one may argue that the touch was less unobtrusive than it appeared, and readers should remember this as well.

If, in closing, I may allow Christopher to speak for himself, here is how he described the difficulties of turning the disorganized collection of "Silmarillion" texts into a single, coherent *Silmarillion* shortly after he had completed the effort:

> To bring it into publishable form was a task at once utterly absorbing and alarming in its responsibility toward something that is unique. To decide what that form should be was not easy; and for a time I worked toward a book that would show something of this diversity, this unfinished and many-branched growth. But it became clear to me that the result would be so complex as to require much study for its comprehension; and I

feared to crush *The Silmarillion* under the weight of its own history. I set myself, therefore, to work out a single text, by selection and arrangement. To give even an impression of the way this has been done is scarcely possible in a short space, and it must suffice to say that in the result *The Silmarillion* is emphatically my father's book and in no sense mine. Here and there I had to develop the narrative out of notes and rough drafts; I had to make many choices between competing versions and to make many changes of detail; and in the last few chapters (which had been left almost untouched for many years) I had in places to modify the narrative to make it coherent. But essentially what I have done has been a work of organization, not of completion.
(Christopher Tolkien 1977: [4])

For good or ill – and I would argue that, for the most part, it is for the good – I think Christopher's assertion that the "*The Silmarillion* is emphatically my father's book and in no sense mine" is not altogether accurate. However, that *The Silmarillion* is, in its essential character, his father's work cannot be disputed, and if Christopher's contributions to its making were his own and not his father's, then their final success for us as readers merely goes to the point that Christopher was indeed his father's son. On the other hand, one must conclude that the book's "difficult" nature must also be attributed, at least in part, to the work of its editor, and the most sensitive readers will remember that the published *Silmarillion* more accurately represents a daunting complex of choices – some of them fortuitous, others missteps – but in this, too, Christopher was clearly his father's son.

JASON FISHER, an independent scholar from Dallas, TX, was educated at Texas A&M University in English, Philosophy, and Psychology. Most recently, Jason has written a series of articles for *The J.R.R. Tolkien Encyclopedia: Scholarship and Critical Assessment* (edited by Michael D.C. Drout, Routledge, 2006) and a chapter on Free Will and Providence in *Tolkien and Modernity* (edited by Thomas Honegger and Frank Weinreich, Walking Tree Publishers, 2006). In addition, Jason has presented papers on J.R.R. Tolkien and the Inklings in a variety of academic settings and conferences.

References

Carpenter, Humphrey, 1977, *Tolkien: A Biography*, Boston: Houghton Mifflin.

Fisher, Jason, 2006, 'Silmarils', in Michael D.C. Drout (ed.), 2006, *J.R.R. Tolkien Encyclopedia: Scholarship and Critical Assessment*, New York: Routledge, pp. 612-13.

Flieger, Verlyn, 2004, 'A Mythology for Finland: Tolkien and Lönnrot as Mythmakers', in Jane Chance (ed.), 2004, *Tolkien and the Invention of Myth*, Lexington, Kentucky: The University Press of Kentucky, pp. 277-283.

Gardner, John, 'The World of Tolkien', in *The New York Times*, 23 October 1977.

Garth, John, 2003, *Tolkien and the Great War: The Threshold of Middle-earth*, Boston: Houghton Mifflin.

Gay, David Elton, 2004, 'J.R.R. Tolkien and the Kalevala: Some Thoughts on the Finnish Origins of Tom Bombadil and Treebeard', in Jane Chance (ed.), 2004, *Tolkien and the Invention of Myth*, Lexington, Kentucky: The University Press of Kentucky, pp. 295-304.

Gilson, Christopher, 1999, '*Narqelion* and the Early Lexicons: Some Notes on the First Elvish Poem', in *Vinyar Tengwar* 40, April 1999, pp. 6-32.

Hammond, Wayne G. and Christina Scull, 1995, *J.R.R. Tolkien: Artist and Illustrator*, Boston: Houghton Mifflin.

——, 2005, *The Lord of the Rings: A Reader's Companion*, Boston: Houghton Mifflin.

Helms, Randel, 1981, *Tolkien and the Silmarils*, Boston: Houghton Mifflin.

Himes, Jonathan B., 2000, 'What Tolkien Really Did with the Sampo', in *Mythlore* 22.4, 2000, pp. 69-85.

Isaacs, Neil D., 2004, 'On the Pleasures of (Reading and Writing) Tolkien Criticism', in Rose A. Zimbardo and Neil D. Isaacs (eds.), 2004, *Understanding The Lord of the Rings: The Best of Tolkien Criticism*, Boston: Houghton Mifflin, pp. 1-10.

Kelly, J.N.D., 1998, *Jerome: His Life, Writings and Controversies*, Peabody, Massachusetts: Hendrickson Publishers.

Kilby, Clyde, 1977, *Tolkien and the Silmarillion*, (first U.K. edition), Berkhamsted: Lion Publishing.

Kocher, Paul, 1980, *A Reader's Guide to The Silmarillion*, London: Thames and Hudson.

Lönnrot, Elias, 1963, *The Kalevala*, (translated by Francis Peabody Magoun, Jr.), Cambridge, Massachusetts: Harvard University Press.

Matthews, Richard, 1978, *Lightning from a Clear Sky*, San Bernardino, California: The Borgo Press. (The Milford Series, Popular Writers of Today: Volume 15)

Nagy, Gergely, 2006, 'Silmarillion', in Michael D.C. Drout (ed.), 2006, *J.R.R. Tolkien Encyclopedia: Scholarship and Critical Assessment*, New York: Routledge, pp. 608-12.

Noad, Charles E., 2000, 'On the Construction of "The Silmarillion"', in Verlyn Flieger and Carl F. Hostetter (eds.), 2000, *Tolkien's Legendarium*, Westport, Connecticut: Greenwood Press, pp. 31-68.

Petty, Anne C., 2004, 'Identifying England's Lönnrot', in *Tolkien Studies* 1, 2004, pp. 69-84.

Purtill, Richard, 1984, *J.R.R. Tolkien: Myth, Morality, and Religion*, San Francisco: Harper and Row.

Scull, Christina and Wayne G. Hammond, 2006, *The J.R.R. Tolkien Companion and Guide: Reader's Guide*, Boston: Houghton Mifflin.

Shippey, Tom, 2000, *J.R.R. Tolkien: Author of the Century*, Boston: Houghton Mifflin.

——, 2003, *The Road to Middle-earth: How J.R.R. Tolkien Created a New Mythology*, (revised and expanded edition, second edition 1992, first edition 1982), Boston: Houghton Mifflin.

Tolkien, Christopher, 1977, *The Silmarillion [by] J.R.R. Tolkien: A Brief Account of the Book and its Making*, [Boston]: Houghton Mifflin.

Tolkien, J.R.R, 1977, *The Silmarillion*, (edited by Christopher Tolkien), Boston: Houghton Mifflin.

——, 1980, *Unfinished Tales of Númenor and Middle-earth*, (edited by Christopher Tolkien), Boston: Houghton Mifflin.

——, 1981, *The Letters of J.R.R. Tolkien*, (selected and edited by Humphrey Carpenter, with assistance from Christopher Tolkien), Boston: Houghton Mifflin.

——, 1984a, *The Book of Lost Tales, Part One*, (edited by Christopher Tolkien), Boston: Houghton Mifflin.

—, 1984b, *The Book of Lost Tales, Part Two*, (edited by Christopher Tolkien), Boston: Houghton Mifflin.

—, 1987, *The Lost Road and Other Writings: Language and Legend before 'The Lord of the Rings'*, (edited by Christopher Tolkien), Boston: Houghton Mifflin.

—, 1992, *Sauron Defeated*, (edited by Christopher Tolkien), Boston: Houghton Mifflin.

—, 1994, *The War of the Jewels: The Later Silmarillion Part Two* (edited by Christopher Tolkien), Boston: Houghton Mifflin.

—, 1995, *Letters from Father Christmas*, (revised edition, edited by Baillie Tolkien), Boston: Houghton Mifflin.

—, 1998, 'The Qenya Lexicon', ed. by Christopher Gilson, Carl F. Hostetter, Patrick Wynne, and Arden R. Smith, in *Parma Eldalamberon* 12, 1998, pp. 29-106.

—, 2004, *The Lord of the Rings*, (50th anniversary edition, first edition 1954-55), Boston: Houghton Mifflin.

Unwin, Rayner, 2000, 'Early Days of Elder Days', in Verlyn Flieger and Carl F. Hostetter (eds.), 2000, *Tolkien's Legendarium*, Westport, Connecticut: Greenwood Press, pp. 3-6.

West, Richard C., 2004, 'Setting the Rocket Off in Story: The Kalevala as the Germ of Tolkien's Legendarium', in Jane Chance (ed.), 2004, *Tolkien and the Invention of Myth*, Lexington, Kentucky: The University Press of Kentucky, pp. 285-294.

Viewpoints, Audiences and Lost Texts in *The Silmarillion**

NILS IVAR AGØY

Abstract

If, while not forgetting Christopher Tolkien's warnings in the foreword to *The Silmarillion*, but knowing also that the book is the chief source of 'information' about the First Age for many Tolkien readers, we nevertheless read it as a collection of 'lost texts', which and whose viewpoints will we find? After sketching the empoemic transmission story of the 'Silmarillion' material through its two main stages – first as Elvish traditions told to Men; later as more or less unreliable human traditions and mythical guesses – the article attempts to answer this. A close reading indicates that it is meant for a Mannish audience with no previous or 'true' information about the Elves, the Valar or the Elder Days, although the focus of attention is still strangely Elvish. The viewpoint is constantly shifting, and narrators pretending to very different levels of knowledge are present, creating such discrepancies that the text cannot function as a Middle-earth representation of 'truth'. The widespread notion that *The Silmarillion* is part of Bilbo's 'Translations from the Elvish' is not supported. For the published *Silmarillion*, the familiar 'lost text technique' simply does not work. More enjoyment is likely to be got from simply regarding it as a mount for the three 'great tales' of the Elder Days.

Do you remember the fox in *The Lord of the Rings*? In the chapter 'Three is Company' he is surprised to find three hobbits sleeping out of doors, "but he never found out any more about it" (Tolkien 2004: 72). He has become famous because *The Lord of the Rings* is overwhelmingly a third-person account, supposedly written by Bilbo, Frodo and Sam, and this is a very rare deviation from that mode, introducing into the text a perspective, a

---

* The author is grateful to Magne Bergland and Allan Turner for comments on draft versions.

viewpoint, which the three hobbits simply could not, on the premises of the story, have known about. Which and whose viewpoints and perspectives can we find in *The Silmarillion*?

J.R.R. Tolkien "came to conceive *The Silmarillion* as a compilation, a compendious narrative, made long afterwards from sources of great diversity (poems, and annals, and oral tales) that had survived in age-long tradition", Christopher Tolkien informs us in the foreword to the book. And when we read *The History of Middle-earth*, we find that the 'lost text technique', the pretence that the work in front of the reader is not really written by a modern author, but consists of translations and retellings of texts far older, is used on the majority of legendarium texts.[1] It is of course used for *The Lord of the Rings*. The technique has many functions, the most important of which – besides giving great pleasure to Tolkien himself – is that it lends verisimilitude to the works, makes the reader's suspension of disbelief easier by blurring the line between fact and fiction. And it stimulates the reader to interact with the texts, drawing inferences, making connections, comparing versions and points of view.

As *The History of Middle-earth* attests, Tolkien went to extreme lengths to present his legendarium as lost texts. His correspondence with readers shows that he was fully prepared to discuss his own books as lost texts, too. In this article, we shall play Tolkien's game with the three texts in the published *Silmarillion* which deal with the events of the First Age: the *Ainulindalë*, the *Valaquenta* and the *Quenta Silmarillion*.[2] If we read it as he wanted it to be read, as a translation of 'lost texts', how do these texts appear? If the book is seen as a compilation of sources, what were the sources like? Can we find out who wrote or told them? Can they be placed? In time? Geographically? Culturally? What was their function?

---

[1] The technique (although not called there by this name) is discussed in some detail in Noad 2000 and Flieger 2005, particularly ch. 4; cf. also Turner 2005 (the sections on 'pseudotranslation'). On shifting points of view in the legendarium, see also Flieger 1997b.

[2] As Christopher Tolkien states in the foreword, the other texts in the published book, the *Akallabêth* and *Of the Rings of Power* are "wholly separate and independent".

But is not this a futile exercise? As we know, *The Silmarillion* as published in 1977 was not a book completed by Tolkien himself, but edited from unfinished manuscripts by his son Christopher. He explicitly warns us in the foreword that the book contains "differences in tone and portrayal, some obscurities, and [...] some lack of cohesion" (Tolkien 1977: 8). And now, with *The History of Middle-earth* complete, it would be possible to reconstruct much of what Christopher Tolkien actually did when he hammered out the text of *The Silmarillion*. Armed with posthumously published manuscripts and notes, supplemented by not a few retrospective reflections on the editorial process by Christopher, we could make many informed guesses as to what *The Silmarillion* would have looked like, had the elder Tolkien finished it.[3] We could list and analyze the many differences between it and the 1977 text, investigate whether or to what extent the elder Tolkien's intentions were reflected, and so on. So, why waste effort on a book which certainly does not reflect its author's ultimate view, and which its editor admits is not fully consistent with the books published in the author's lifetime? The answer, of course, is that the 1977 text has a far larger audience than the exceedingly complicated welter of texts in *The History of Middle-earth*. For the great majority of Tolkien readers, it is the standard, authoritative source of 'information' about the Elder Days. For good or ill it actually works as a collection of 'lost texts' alongside *The Lord of the Rings* and *The Hobbit*, and it is therefore of interest to take a closer look at how it functions when read in this way.

The 1977 text, not the myriad of texts in *The History of Middle-earth*, is therefore the object of our investigation. It must nevertheless be legitimate to take a quick look back at the development of the legendarium. Not to let the earlier texts condition our reading of the newer, which should be as assumption-free as possible, but to help us narrow down the scope of our investigation by revealing what main functions *The Silmarillion* was

---

[3] Charles Noad has made an excellent start in his article 'On the Construction of "The Silmarillion"' (Noad 2000).

intended by its author to have. There were two of these. First, it was to provide a framework for telling the 'great tales' which, along with a string of vividly imagined and curiously stable dramatic tableaux or episodes, were primary/pre-existing in Tolkien's mind; the book would provide a narrative thread on which these pearls could be hung.[4] Second, it was to provide some explanation or indication of how the material had been transmitted, so that it has reached us modern readers. It is this second function, namely transmission, that is immediately relevant in our connection, because Tolkien always, in all the different versions, chose to use some variant of the 'lost text technique'.

Earlier versions of the 'Silmarillion' material are on the whole, for all their fluctuations and permutations, much easier to handle as 'lost texts' than the 1977 text because they often contain explicit statements about their own supposed provenance. From the 1926 *Sketch of the Mythology*, intended to give R.W. Reynolds sufficient background to understand the story of the Children of Húrin, through the 1930s, the 1940s and much of the 1950s, the provenance story was basically the same: The material was told and/or shown by the Elves of Tol Eressëa to Eriol/Ælfwine, a man from Britain (in a wide sense) in the Middle Ages (the dates vary) who managed both to reach the Lonely Isle and get back again alive. According to this scheme, *The Silmarillion* consisted of almost purely Elvish traditions, but was translated (in the more developed versions) by an Anglo-Saxon for the use of other humans. Alongside the Ælfwine story, there was also present a much weaker, but still explicit, notion that the stories are still sung and told by "the fading Elves" (who may presumably still be encountered in the Hither Lands), and that they tell them at times to "Men of the race of Eärendel".[5]

---

[4] Cf. C. Tolkien 1977, Tolkien 1981: 360, and Agøy 1987.

[5] 1926 *Sketch* (Tolkien 1986: 41): "These tales are some of those remembered and sung by the fading Elves, and most by the vanished Elves of the Lonely Isle. They have been told by Elves to Men of the race of Eärendel, and most to Eriol who alone of mortals of later days sailed to the Lonely Isle, and yet came back to Lúthien, [Britain or England] and remembered things he had heard in Cortirion, the town of the Elves in Tol Eressëa."

1930 *Silmarillion* (Tolkien 1986: 165): "Some of these things are sung and said yet by the fading Elves, and more still are sung by the vanished Elves that dwell now on the Lonely Isle. To Men of the race of Eärendel have they at times been told, and most to

This basic scheme was confirmed by a letter from Tolkien to Katherine Farrer (Tolkien 1981: 130) as late as 1948, when most of *The Lord of the Rings* had been written.⁶ The notion that the legends of the First Age were transmitted by Ælfwine even survived the publication of *The Lord of the Rings* in 1954-55, as can be seen from the two texts reproduced in Tolkien 1993: 311-315. This is rather surprising, as it is strongly hinted in the 'Note on the Shire Records' in *The Lord of the Rings* that the Red Book of Westmarch, on which it is supposedly based, had been preserved in Middle-earth, and among Men (including Hobbits). One would have thought that the publication of *The Lord of the Rings*, where the 'Silmarillion' traditions are referred to, would have stimulated Tolkien to invent a scheme whereby both *The Lord of the Rings* and *The Silmarillion* had come to modern readers from the same source, especially as we know that he originally wanted both works to be published together. In practice, one might

---

Eriol, who alone of the mortals of later days, and yet now long ago, sailed to the Lonely Isle, and came back to Leithien where he lived, and remembered things that he had heard in fair Cortirion, the city of the Elves in Tol Eressëa."

1937 *Silmarillion* (Tolkien 1987: 201 and 333f.) : "...a history in brief drawn from many older tales; for all the matters that it contains were of old, and still are among the Eldar of the West, recounted more fully in other histories and songs. But many of these were not recalled by Eriol, or men have lost them again since his day. This Account was composed first by Pengolod of Gondolin, and Ælfwine turned it into our speech as it was in his time"; "...drawn out in brief from those songs and histories which are yet sung and told by the fading Elves, and (more clearly and fully) by the vanished Elves that dwell now upon the Lonely Isle, Tol Eressëa, whither few mariners of Men have ever come, save once or twice in a long age when some man of Eärendel's race hath passed beyond the lands of mortal sight and seen the glimmer of the lamps of Avallon, and smelt afar the undying flowers in the meads of Dorwinion. Of whom was Eriol one, that men named Ælfwine, and he alone returned and brought tidings of Cortirion to the Hither Lands."

6   Although Ælfwine was not mentioned, Tolkien also confirmed in his letter to Milton Waldman in (?) 1951 that "the point of view of the whole cycle [the legendarium stories of the Elder Days] is the Elvish"; "the legendary *Silmarillion* [...] differs from all similar things that I know in not being anthropocentric. Its centre of view and interest is not Men but 'Elves'" (Tolkien 1981: 147).

Following the introduction of Númenor into Tolkien's legendarium in the 1930s, we find him experimenting in the 1940s, in *The Lost Road* and *The Notion Club Papers*, with very different modes of transmission, such as time travel and inherited memories. However, this work does not seem to have had any significant impact on his conception of the transmission of the basic Silmarillion material, and so we will not go into it in detail here. Interested readers are referred to Noad 2000 and Flieger 1997a.

have expected him to either abandon the Ælfwine story and explicitly identify *The Silmarillion* with parts of Bilbo's 'Translations from the Elvish' instead; or, if the Ælfwine story was to remain the explanation of how the books have reached us, to somehow place the Red Book in Tol Eressëa, so that Ælfwine could have found it there. He did neither.[7] A reminder Tolkien wrote to himself in a copy of the first edition of *The Fellowship of the Ring* (which did not contain the 'Note on the Shire Records') does show that, at some point between 1954 and 1965, he wished to present the unfinished Silmarillion as one of Bilbo's translations, or at least as a work transmitted by the hobbits. He stated that the 'Note on the Shire Records' should not be included in *The Fellowship of the Ring*: "It belongs to Preface to *The Silmarillion*" (Tolkien 1996: 14). He seems, however, to have changed his mind, for the 'Note on the Shire Records' was in fact printed in the second edition of *The Fellowship of the Ring* in 1965. On the reasons for this, we can only speculate. He may have realized that he would not be able to finish *The Silmarillion* for a considerable time, but wanted his readers to have

---

[7] *The Silmarillion* is mentioned in *The Lord of the Rings*, but only in Appendix A and F, not in the narrative. The parts of the appendices not placed in quotation marks were supposedly formulated by Tolkien in his role as the modern-day translator-editor of the work, who based his work mainly, but not exclusively, on the sources mentioned in the 'Note on the Shire Records', among which the Red Book was the most important. The mention of *The Silmarillion* comes in the sections outside quotation marks and thus the only conclusion to be drawn is that it was known to the translator-editor.

In the introduction to Appendix A, it is said that Bilbo's chief interest lay in the ancient legends of the First Age. Many readers have assumed (and some have assumed without question) that *The Silmarillion* formed part of Bilbo's 'Translations from the Elvish'. The assumption is probably based mainly on the statement, in the 'Note on the Shire Records' in the Prologue to *The Lord of the Rings*, that these translations were "almost entirely concerned with the Elder Days". Cf. Tolkien 1983: 5-6, where Christopher Tolkien writes that, when preparing the 1977 text, he assumed that his father had intended *The Silmarillion* to be one of Bilbo's 'Translations from the Elvish', adding that he had later come to regret not having made "definite what I only surmised". Cf. also Noad 2000: 55, touching on Tolkien's view of the relationship between *The Lord of the Rings* and the Ælfwine story in the mid-1950s. Noad notes that it is remarkable that the *Akallabêth* was mentioned in the first edition of *The Lord of the Rings*, as it was "a text that Tolkien had only recently made" and one that implicitly referred to Pengoloð, an elfsage of Tol Eressëa, and to Ælfwine. The direct reference to the *Akallabêth*, said to be held among the records of Gondor, was removed from later editions of *The Lord of the Rings*. See also Noad 2000: 57, 65 (where Noad accepts the transmission of *The Silmarillion* through the Red Book).

On the evolution of the Red Book, see also Flieger 2006.

some account of the provenance of *The Lord of the Rings* in the meantime. He may also have realized that a direct attribution of *The Silmarillion* to Bilbo would entail a major reworking of it, for reasons touched on later in this article. Inclusion of the note in *The Silmarillion* would have tied that work directly to the Red Book, but its inclusion in *The Lord of the Rings* did not give the same result, as it does not actually name *The Silmarillion*. Nevertheless, he kept his options open. In 1966, he told Richard Plotz that he was "considering" (but note, only considering) "making use of Bilbo again" in the sense that *The Silmarillion* might "perhaps" appear as Bilbo's research in Rivendell (Plotz 1967: 118). As we shall see, it is important to keep in mind that this refers to an unwritten Silmarillion, not the 1977 text.

For Tolkien never stopped struggling with the unfinished book. In 1958 (? – the year is not certain) cosmological considerations finally convinced him to discard both Ælfwine and the notion that the 'Silmarillion' material was almost purely Elvish – because the High Elves from whom Ælfwine had his information would know better than to pass on 'primitive' astronomical notions which were squarely at odds with the observed facts of the 20th century, but which figure in *The Silmarillion*. Men, however, without direct access to the demiurgic Valar, might be expected to harbour all kinds of 'primitive' notions. So in a series of highly interesting notes, Tolkien concluded that the mythology "must actually be a 'Mannish' affair":

> What we have in the *Silmarillion* etc. are traditions (especially personalized, and centred upon *actors*, such as Fëanor) handed on by *Men* in Númenor and later in Middle-earth (Arnor and Gondor); but already far back – from the first association of the Dúnedain and Elf-friends with the Eldar in Beleriand – blended and confused with their own Mannish myths and cosmic ideas.
> (Tolkien 1993: 370)

The three great tales of *The Silmarillion* (i.e. about Beren, Túrin, and Tuor/Eärendil) "must be Númenorean, and derived from matter preserved in

Gondor" (Tolkien 1993: 373). He further commented that the mythology is represented as

> being two stages removed from a true record: it is first based upon Elvish records and lore about the Valar and their own dealings with them; and these have reached us (fragmentarily) only through relics of Númenórean (human) traditions, derived from the Eldar, in the earlier parts, though for later times supplemented by anthropocentric histories and tales. These, it is true, came down through the 'Faithful' and their descendants in Middle-earth, but could not altogether escape the darkening of the picture due to the hostility of the rebellious Númenóreans to the Valar".
> (Tolkien 1993: 401f.)

This new scheme represented a drastic and intended loss of assumed credibility (i.e. credibility in the universe described in the books). Instead of almost pure and (one must believe) highly reliable Elvish traditions, based on information from the Valar, personal experience, first-hand sources and millennia of Elvish scholarship, we would have muddled and biased Mannish traditions, including human 'mythical guesses'.[8]

This remained the elder Tolkien's view of the pretended provenance of the material in *The Silmarillion*. In a work probably deriving from the late 1960s (definitely after February 1968, but not possible to date more accurately) he stated unequivocally that *The Silmarillion*

---

[8] Tolkien 1993: 389. Cf. Tolkien's notes to the commentary on *Athrabeth Finrod ah Andreth*, especially note 2 and 7: Tolkien 1993: 337-339 and 342-343. The notes were probably written in 1959. Among other things, Tolkien discusses the nature and reliability of Elvish and Mannish traditions, particularly in relation to "Men's present [i.e. 20th century] theories". Referring to cosmology, he notes that "[n]ot everything is adumbrated in the *Ainulindalë*; or the *Ainulindalë* may have a wider reference than we knew" (338). Furthermore: "The myth that appears at the end of the *Silmarillion* [the Prophecy of Mandos, found in Tolkien 1987: 333] is of Númenórean origin; it is clearly made by Men, though men acquainted with Elvish tradition" (342).

is not an Eldarin title or work. It is a compilation, probably made in Númenor, which includes (in prose) the four great tales or lays of the heroes of the Atani, of which 'The Children of Húrin' was probably composed already in Beleriand in the First Age, but necessarily is preceded by an account of Fëanor and the making of the Silmarils. All however are 'Mannish' works.
(Tolkien 1996: 357, note 17)[9]

And in a note probably written in the last year of his life, he stated, when discussing "a false notion, e.g. probably of Mannish origin" that "nearly all the matter of *The Silmarillion* is contained in myths and legends that have passed through Men's hands and minds, and are (in many points) plainly influenced by contact and confusion with the myths, theories, and legends of Men".[10]

It should be noted that at least the first of these two late writings was used when the published *Silmarillion* was prepared, and so presumably influenced Christopher Tolkien during his editorial work.[11] It should also be noted that the transmission of 'lost texts' from the first three ages of Middle-earth to 20th century Europe was never completely explained in any work published in Tolkien's lifetime. He never explained how or in what form the

---

[9] In *The Adventures of Tom Bombadil*, published in 1962, there is reference to "the High-elvish and Númenorean legends of Eärendil", and to the idea that Númenorean lore, including traditions about Túrin and Mîm, was preserved in Rivendell (Tolkien 1962: 8). Also present is the notion that "Southern matter", i.e. from Gondor, might have reached Bilbo "by way of Rivendell".

[10] Tolkien 1996: 390, note 17. Cf. Tolkien 1981: 411, where, referring to *The Lord of the Rings* and *The Silmarillion* both, he told a friend in 1971 that "the legends are mainly of 'Mannish' origin blended with those of the Sindar (Gray-elves) and others who had never left Middle-earth."

[11] Tolkien 1996: 331. – Some years later, in the foreword to *The Book of Lost Tales* (Tolkien 1983: 5), Christopher Tolkien wrote that he thought his father had in the end concluded that no "device" or "framework" for the presentation of the legends of the Elder Days "would serve, and no more would be said beyond an explanation of how (within the imagined world) it came to be recorded." Although written at the start of the work on *The History of Middle-earth*, this is not contradicted by the late notes just referred to, which can be taken to deal only with the transmission of the legends "within the imagined world". Cf. Noad 2000: 32.

Red Book of Westmarch had survived to modern times. And even in his unpublished work, many links in the chain of transmission are missing.

We now turn to the published *Silmarillion*. Familiarity with its contents is assumed in the following.

A. Ainulindalë

No author or editor or transmitter or translator presents him- or herself in the *Ainulindalë* itself (but see the next paragraph), and no explanation is given as to why or for whom it was written. Nevertheless, it seems very unlikely that it was made for the Eldar, for they are observed as it were from the outside. We see it in such formulations as "even the Eldar cannot clearly perceive" the Valar when they walk unclad (Tolkien 1977: 21) or references to what "is told among the Eldar" (Tolkien 1977: 22). The supposed audience is practically invisible. The readers are directly referred to only once, where it is stated on p. 21 that "we" normally wear raiment – which does not really help very much in deciding who "we" are. And when we are told about "that Ainu whom the Elves call Ulmo" without any other name being given, this suggests that the audience has no equivalent name. Further we may note that the target culture is acquainted with organs (the musical instruments). This suggests a certain level of cultural and technological sophistication, but certainly not above that of Númenor or Gondor, and hardly above that of late Anglo-Saxon Britain. When, however, the narrative voice invites the audience to consider the Earth in relation to the World (in this context: the universe), and stresses its seeming insignificance, s/he assumes a level of astronomical knowledge and a philosophical outlook that seem much more at home in the 20th century than in the Middle Ages or among Men of the Third Age. Or more at home in Aman – we could of course assume this invitation to be taken over directly from the wise and profound Eldar.

A complication arises in that the *Ainulindalë* is attributed to the elf-sage Rúmil of Tirion in the *Silmarillion* index. This attribution is of course likely to be taken as 'fact' by most readers, but as we have just seen, there are features in the text itself which militate against it. The easiest way out is probably to regard the text as it now stands as a Mannish adaptation of Rúmil's original. (This also fits in with earlier conceptions in *The History of Middle-earth*, where versions of Rúmil's *Ainulindalë* were written down by Ælfwine.[12])

The information contained in the *Ainulindalë* is said to "come from the Valar themselves, with whom the Eldalië spoke in the land of Valinor, and by whom they were instructed" (Tolkien 1977: 22). Nevertheless, for large stretches of text, the viewpoint is neither Elvish or Valarian, but something outside them both. The narrative voice begins its story before the Ainur were created. It claims to know not only the thoughts of several Ainur, including Melkor, but also what Eru did when He was alone, and what He then thought. Presuming that the text is meant to be accepted as 'true', a trustworthy description of the creation of the world (calling it a 'myth' does not dispel the difficulty), the only possible source of such information is Eru himself. The inference is that we should see these parts of the texts as divine revelation (perhaps in the same way as many Christians see Genesis, where a similar knowledge of God's mind is present). In light of the remark just cited, we are probably meant to assume that He has revealed His thoughts to some of the Valar, not to an Elf or Man (and if He had, we would expect the circumstances to be mentioned). This would in any case fit in with Eru's overall remoteness in the legendarium[13].

Alternatively we could see it as the Narrator's pious attempt to understand and explain the Creation, as one view among many. Nevertheless, the theory that the knowledge of Eru's actions and thoughts is to be regarded as true revelation rather than pious or mythopoeic speculation is strengthened by the fact that the text openly admits lack of knowledge on some subjects. "[L]ittle would the Valar ever tell of the wars before the coming of the Elves", the narrative voice informs us, before immediately attempting to paper over this hole in certain knowledge with Elvish

---

[12] See for instance Tolkien 1987: 156; Tolkien 1993: 30.
[13] Cf. Flieger 2005: 140.

conjecture: "Yet it is told among the Eldar…" (Tolkien 1977: 22) Another conjecture ("…it has been said…") concerns the "greater music" after the end of days (Tolkien 1977: 15).

For all its dependence on the Valar, the narrative voice is able to view and evaluate the Ainur from above, so to speak, and is strangely mindful of their limitations. Some "things there are", the narrative voice states, "that they cannot see, neither alone nor taking counsel together; for to none but himself has Ilúvatar revealed all that he has in store" (Tolkien 1977: 18). The statement that Manwë and Ulmo "in all things have served most faithfully the purpose of Ilúvatar" (Tolkien 1977: 19) also takes an external view of the Valar.

The *Ainulindalë* cannot be dated beyond the obvious fact that it must belong to a time after Men have come into contact with Elves who had, directly or indirectly, traditions from Aman.

B. VALAQUENTA

The *Valaquenta*, too, is anonymously given "according to the lore of the Eldar" (Tolkien 1977: 25), and the names of the Valar and Valier are explicitly given in Valinorean form. Again, the contents are Elvish, but the audience is clearly not. Again, the viewpoint is lofty, presuming to assess the Valar and list their strengths and weaknesses; and again, it seems clear that the audience is assumed to know nothing or next to nothing about the subject matter. We are told that "Men have often named [the Valar] gods", and that "their names among Men are manifold" (Tolkien 1977: 25). If the *Valaquenta* was intended for a specific human society, we would strongly expect examples of these names to appear ('Now Ulmo is the god that we call Njord', or similar), but this does not happen. Possibly this could be taken to means that the text was written down as heard or simply copied out of an Elvish book of lore, with only a few additions made, i.e. the third-person comments on and information about the Elves (e.g. "…the Elves hold Varda most in reverence and love. Elbereth they call her, and they call upon her name out of the shadows of Middle-earth"; Tolkien 1977: 26).

The *Valaquenta* refers to "histories of the Elder Day" (Tolkien 1977: 30) and also notes that Sauron "rose like a shadow of Morgoth and a ghost of his malice" (Tolkien 1977: 32). Thus it could, in Middle-earth terms, hardly date from earlier than the middle of the Second Age, when Sauron had declared himself. It mentions the *Quenta Silmarillion* by name and therefore has to date from the same time as this, or be younger. The reference may be an indication that the two works were intended to supplement each other.

C. QUENTA SILMARILLION

This long and uneven text is not attributed to any author or transmitter either, but it does show clear signs of editorial work: there are references back[14] and forth,[15] as well as declarations that the material presented is thematically selected from a much larger mass. Nevertheless, for a work entitled 'The History of the Silmarils', there is a remarkable amount of material where the Silmarils do not figure either directly or indirectly. In particular, the long and detailed story of Túrin does not really defend its place in such a history.

The viewpoint of the anonymous Narrator is very detached. There are no observations in the first tense, and information is often introduced in a curiously impersonal and non-committal manner: "It is said", "It is told", "Some say".

The narrative voice exhibits a striking mix of limited knowledge and seeming omniscience. In many instances, it speaks with total authority. It tells us not only what human or elvish characters feel and think and know, or even what the Valar think and say to one another, but, as in the *Ainulindalë*, about Eru's thoughts and actions (e.g. Tolkien 1977: 41f.). The Narrator can state, with no discernible modesty, that Manwë, the Lord of the near-divine Valar, "saw not to the depths of Melkor's heart" (Tolkien 1977: 66), while he himself, by contrast, is often able to tell exactly what Melkor/Morgoth

---

[14] E.g. Tolkien 1977: 55, 91, 94, 95, 118, 126, 183, 242.
[15] Tolkien 1977: 53, 55, 161.

thinks, what his intentions are, what he remembers, and so on.[16] This is remarkable both because there seems to be no way of *knowing* this on the premises of the text, short of a new revelation from Eru – one hardly imagines Morgoth giving interviews prior to being thrust through the Door of Night, and by the nature of things, not even the Valar could read Morgoth's mind – and because of a number of opposing statements regarding the impossibility of having just this kind of knowledge: "For who of the living has descended into the pits of Utumno, or has explored the darkness of the counsels of Melkor", the Narrator asks; and "Who knows now the counsels of Morgoth? Who can measure the reach of his thought" (Tolkien 1977: 50 and 205).[17] Similarly, he rules out, contrary to many of his own statements elsewhere, the possibility of reporting Manwë's mind: "of the counsels of his heart what tale shall tell" (Tolkien 1977: 244)? In another group of statements, the Narrator relies on *reports* about Morgoth's reactions: "It is said that hate overcame his counsel"; "it is said that Morgoth looked not for the assault that came upon him" (Tolkien 1977: 150 and 250; see also 153).

The most obvious inference is that we are dealing with at least two different Narrators, who are voicing different perspectives, probably stemming from different points in time. The issue is however complex. One might have thought that the statements claiming intimate knowledge of the Valar were early, from a time when access to lore from Aman was readily available; while the more reserved statements were later, from an age when unclear points could no longer be cleared up because no ships sailed to Middle-earth from Aman. This would not, however, explain how Morgoth's mind was known. And if one puts the statements claiming knowledge about Morgoth's and Manwë's minds in the same group, as seems reasonable to me, one could rather believe that these were late speculations, written at a time when the Valar themselves seemed infinitely remote and inaccessible,

---

[16] E.g. Tolkien 1977: 36, 51, 65, 66, 67f., 81, 107, 109, 115, 141f., 145, 160, 180, 196, 227, 244, 250.

[17] Cf. p. 106: "No tale has told what Morgoth thought in his heart at the tidings that Fëanor [...] had brought a host out of the West."

and it would not seem presumptuous or maybe even blasphemous to poetically attribute feelings and motives to them.

Setting the inner lives of Morgoth and Manwë aside for the moment, there are many other types of knowledge that it would seem impossible for the Narrator to possess, even if we allow that he may have received information from the Valar and from the Eldar west of the Sea.[18] Who, for instance, listened in on the quarrel between Morgoth and Ungoliant after the rape of the Two Trees, or could observe their behaviour before the rape, in a land explicitly "empty"? Or how could anyone know exactly what was said between Glaurung and Túrin just before they both died? How can the Narrator know what passed in Carcharoth's mind just before he devoured the Silmaril, seeing that he straightaway went mad and was killed soon after? – The most obvious explanation is that poetic license is frequently used to introduce extrapolation, conjecture, and guesswork, with a corresponding loss of textual authority.

Intriguingly, some very few of these instances of 'problematic' knowledge are given other explanations. The account of how hapless Gorlim was questioned and killed by Sauron is provided by his ghost, which appears to Beren. The duel between Fingolfin and Morgoth was reported by the eagle Thorondor. In *The History of Middle-earth* some additional loose threads are wound up – the reason we can know about the battle of Amon Rûdh is because one of Túrin's outlaws, Andróg, survived (as he does not in the published *Silmarillion*) and passed the story on to his son. This seems to indicate that Tolkien himself saw the presence of these types of information as problematic, and wanted to explain it without resorting to the easiest solution, i.e. simply letting the narrative appear as a work of fiction with an all-knowing author.

In a few cases, the Narrator carefully points out things that are not known, and refers to discussions about them. Unclear and debated points in

---

[18] Access to the Eldar of Aman might for instance explain how we could know about Thingol's thoughts just prior to his death. But it is not a really good explanation of how we know about Maedhros' last moments, as he was presumably kept incommunicado in Mandos for many an age.

the *Quenta Silmarillion* are whether Men are a grief to Manwë; Dwarvish afterlife; the origins of Orcs; what would have happened had Finwë not married again; Ungoliant's origins and fate; the effects of Fëanor's refusal to give up the Silmarils to the Valar; why Manwë did not listen to Ulmo's plea to intervene in the fate of Middle-earth after the fall of Gondolin; and Tuor's final fate. We may note that several of the uncertain points have to do with metaphysics/death/afterlife; i.e. questions that maybe even the Valar do not have clear answers to.[19] But some are prosaic: "Some say" that the messenger from Manwë confronting the fleeing Noldor on the borders of Araman was Mandos himself (Tolkien 1977: 87). But if this was important enough to argue about, why would not the Valar settle the question, seeing that they yielded up much information of much the same sort in other contexts?

The Narrator quite frequently refers to other works, either as sources or as places where additional information may be found. These works may be written (including the *Ainulindalë*) or oral. The references seem rather to express the Narrator's wish to show the audience that there is much lore to draw upon than any wish to bolster his own trustworthiness by claiming that the sources he uses are more reliable than others. The sources are overwhelmingly Elvish. And at the end of the *Quenta Silmarillion* it is strongly suggested that the "Elves who had dwelt and suffered in the Hither Lands, and who made the histories of those days that are still known" are the main sources of information (Tolkien 1977: 251). In the same place it is implied that this limits the information available in the work: little is known about the march of the host of the Valar to the north of Middle-earth at the end of the First Age because none of these Elves went among them, "and tidings of these things they only learned long afterwards from their kinsfolk in Aman". Taken literally, this tells us that the information, "tidings of these things" is available to the Beleriandic Elves who made the histories now, but that it has not yet been incorporated into those same histories or into the *Quenta* itself.

---

[19] And – to leave the empoemic mode for a moment – about which J.R.R. Tolkien never made up his mind.

It is not easy to see why this should be so, seeing that much other information which must necessarily have come from Elves who never left Aman is actually present in the *Quenta*. Anyway, we get the impression that parts of the *Quenta* are composed mainly in the Hither Lands, with little access to information from Aman.[20] This adds to the overall picture of the *Quenta* as an uneven, compendious work.

As in the *Ainulindalë* and the *Valaquenta*, the audience is invisible, and the viewpoint is predominantly non-Elvish. "Immortal were the Elves", the audience is told – a piece of information unnecessary to any Elf (Tolkien 1977: 104).[21] A chapter-by-chapter analysis of the viewpoint reveals that, although not entirely constant – (who but an Elf could have claimed that the Noontime of the Blessed Realm was "in memory too brief"?[22]) – it is for the most part Mannish. The Narrator is interested in Mannish afterlife, seems proud on behalf of the Edain (see especially p. 105 and 148), gives his readers basic information about the sundering of the Elves (p. 53) and often informs his readers about what the Dwarves and Elves call this or that. Nevertheless, stray comments show that even the Edain are scrutinized in a critical, detached way. They learned "of the Eldar all such art and knowledge as they could receive"; "little have the Valar ever prevailed to sway the wills of Men" (Tolkien 1977: 149, 68). And while the Narrator is able to report in some detail about the motives of the Valar, including their disagreements and secret purposes (e.g. Tolkien 1977: 43, about Aulë making the Dwarves in secret, "fearing that the other Valar might blame his work"), he tells his readers that "Men have feared the Valar, rather than loved them, and have not understood the purposes of the Powers" (Tolkien 1977: 103).

---

[20] Cf. p. 95, where it is said that "much that was held in memory perished in the ruins of Doriath" because the people of that kingdom used Cirth little for the keeping of records. One would have thought that the memories did not really perish, but would still be extant in Aman.

[21] And it does appear as a piece of information rather than as poetic reflection or suchlike.

[22] Tolkien 1977: 63. See also p. 95 with its interesting appeal to common knowledge: Melkor's slaying of the Trees of the Valar and his quarrel with Ungoliant is "known to all, being written in lore and sung in many songs".

As for date, it is clear that the events described belong to a remote past; "many an age" has since passed (Tolkien 1977: 254). There is a direct reference to "the White Tree of Númenor" and it is noted that "the fashion of the world" has since changed (Tolkien 1977: 59, 62). This can hardly be any other than the change described in the *Akallabêth*, and we are thus in the Third Age or later. It is equally clear that the Elves are believed to be still extant; though perhaps only in theory, or in Aman. Some very external descriptions ("Immortal were the elves...") may point to the latter, and seems to indicate that few if any in the audience have ever encountered one. The assertion (in the same chapter) that Men and Elves "were of like stature and strength of body" in those days, also seem to indicate that a very long time has passed, and the Elves have dwindled significantly (Tolkien 1977: 104).

CONCLUSIONS AND CONJECTURES

At least two different narrative voices are present in *Ainulindalë*, *Valaquenta* and *Quenta Silmarillion*:

- one knowing the unknowable, particularly regarding characters' thoughts and motives, like a modern author of fiction;
- one dependent on and limited by Elvish traditions, pointing out where certain knowledge fails.

The second one is of course what we would expect in a work employing the 'lost text technique' and represented as a 'true' account. It should be noted that the two distinct voices are both to be found throughout the book. If the All-knowing Author were to be found, for instance, only in the parts of *Quenta Silmarillion* where the pace is relatively slow (like the tales of Túrin and Beren) s/he might perhaps be written off as Mannish conjecture in sections dealing primarily with Mannish heroes. However, this is not the case.

The discrepancies, and particularly the presence of the All-knowing Author, mean that the published text does come across as a compendium, a mingling of traditions. But it does not come across as a work to be implicitly trusted – its overall authority is questionable because of all the clearly fictional elements. For this reason, the *Quenta Silmarillion* cannot function as a Middle-earth representation of 'truth', as an historical account.

We have seen earlier that Tolkien wanted *The Silmarillion* to give the reader clues as to how the material had been transmitted. How does the 1977 text work in this regard?

The *Ainulindalë*, *Valaquenta* and *Quenta Silmarillion*, when read by themselves as 'lost texts', all appear to be Mannish, but to be derived from mainly Elvish sources.[23] The *Ainulindalë* may stem from the First Age, but the *Quenta Silmarillion* and the *Valaquenta* have to be Third Age or later. According to Appendix F in *The Lord of the Rings*, the *Silmarillion* story of the creation of the Dwarves by Aulë was not known to "the lesser Elves of Middle-earth […] while the tales of later Men are confused with memories of other races" (Tolkien 2004: 1132). It is not possible to determine exactly which elves are meant by this, but presumably we may postulate that the *Silmarillion* was not a work read among the Silvan elves.

We cannot place the texts more definitely either in time or space, but some additional comments may nevertheless be made. For instance, the Elvish bias in the *Quenta Silmarillion* is interesting: even the material on the Edain and the stories of the great human heroes seems to have been transmitted exclusively through the Elves. If the texts as they are printed in *The Silmarillion* had been transmitted for some length of time by Men of the Second or Third Age, we would expect to see traces of Mannish tradition alongside the Elvish versions in this imperfectly edited compendium of many sources. We would expect references to *human* lays and histories, more on the legends and traditions of the Edain before their arrival in

---

[23] It will be seen that I differ from Christopher Tolkien's assertion (C. Tolkien 1977, no pagination) that the story of *The Silmarillion* "is seen largely through Elvish eyes" but am in agreement with J.R.R. Tolkien's post-1958 position as outlined above on pp. 145-147.

Beleriand (something more than just the Elvish tradition that Morgoth had meddled in their early history, Tolkien 1977: 141) and so on. The fact that such material is missing entirely, would seem to make a Númenor/Gondor transmission less likely.

Then there is the nature of the texts to consider. The *Quenta Silmarillion* can function in several ways, but as 'lost texts', both the *Ainulindalë* and the *Valaquenta* claim to convey 'truths' of a religious nature, and the *Valaquenta* in particular introduces the Valar *to a seemingly fully unsuspecting audience*. Instruction in this form would, one suspects, have been unnecessary and therefore unlikely among Men of Third Age Middle-earth, except perhaps for young children. In Gondor, at least, the Valar were known, and if we accept that *The Lord of the Rings* was written by hobbits, they too were sufficiently familiar with the Valar not to have to explain them (there are three references to the Valar in the narrative of *The Lord of the Rings*). And we have seen that the *Valaquenta* and the *Quenta Silmarillion* are connected and possibly intended for the same audience, i.e. one which has apparently never heard of the Valar before.

There are striking parallels between the first part of *The Silmarillion* (particularly the *Ainulindalë* and the opening chapters of the *Quenta Silmarillion*) and Genesis in the Bible: the swift movement from the Creation through a 'mythical' age to 'historical' events; the unabashed and obvious assembly of the text from several sources; the taken-for-granted authority of the narrative voice, even when it speaks of God, i.e. its quality of revelation. But a major difference between the two texts is the tendency in *The Silmarillion* to explain from the bottom up – a clear signal that it is not intended to function in a culture where Eru or Elves or Valar are something known (or objects of faith).

Further, we must take into account the frequent references to other works. The references in themselves do not, of course, mean that the sources cited were still extant, but if they were, we are dealing with a literate society where numerous Elvish works are available. However, this would presuppose a knowledge of Elvish languages (and hence of Elves) that would seem to make many of the basic descriptions and comments on Elves superfluous and/or insulting. A Third Age setting (e.g. in Gondor or Rivendell, or even the Shire) is for this reason improbable. If the works cited were not available to the audience, the references would still have to be there for a reason, and the most likely one is that such references would impress the audience and give authority to the present work. This too points to a fairly sophisticated literary culture, but one with little or no first-hand knowledge of Elves.

The evidence is admittedly slender, but it all points in the same direction: Read as 'lost texts', the 1977 *Silmarillion* seems to be a work meant for a Mannish audience with no previous or 'true' information about either the Elves, the Valar or the history of the Elder Days. This could fit in well enough with the old Ælfwine scheme, but hardly with *The Silmarillion* ever forming part of Bilbo's 'Translations from the Elvish'. And indeed the external view taken of the Elves would seem absurd in a work originally written in "the Elvish". But of course, translation is an imprecise term and could cover much reworking of the original. Bilbo as translator may have intended his work to be read by people much less familiar with Elves (or myths about the Valar) than himself. But if he is responsible for the Mannish bias in *The Silmarillion*, it is strange that there is no trace at all of a Hobbit point of view. Then again he may have translated Mannish texts written *in* Elvish. In that case, his choice of title seems slightly misleading. Also, the 'Note on the Shire Records' explicitly states that Bilbo had made use of all the sources, written or oral, available to him in Rivendell in the preparation of his translations, and it is hard to see why these sources, presumably including Elrond himself and elf-lords like Glorfindel, would result in so Mannish a text.

It could be added that if we accept Tolkien's position that the book contains 'wrong' information about the structure of the world, it could hardly have been transmitted through Ælfwine – one recalls that it was for this very reason that the Ælfwine scheme was discarded. But in such a case it is equally unlikely to have been written or translated by Bilbo using, as just mentioned, all the written and oral sources Rivendell could provide. We may then assume that Elrond and others would have been able to give a more accurate account than the one Tolkien came to see as biased and unduly anthropocentric.[24] On the balance, then, the theory that the 1977 *Silmarillion* formed part of Bilbo's 'Translations from the Elvish' seems unlikely.

THE VIEW FROM OUTSIDE THE LOST TEXT GAME

We started with a promise to look at how *The Silmarillion* functions when read as a collection of 'lost texts'. So, how does it function? The answer must be: Not very well. The main reason for this is, I think, the one that emerges from the preceding pages: The 'lost texts' are simply too lost. It is too unclear who they are for and why they are there. They lack context of the kind that in other parts of the legendarium stimulates the reader to relate to a text or a story in several ways, for its own sake as well as for the light it throws on people or events which we as readers have already become interested in. The context that is actually there is not always easy to see, nor is it in any way firm. The author of these lines first bought *The Silmarillion* on the date of publication in 1977, has read it many times since then and has translated it. Nevertheless, the 'fact' that (to take one example) it is a mainly Mannish work was something I had to deduce – and therefore clearly not something that has been important for my enjoyment of the book.

In this case, then, the 'lost text technique' does not so much provide depth or verisimilitude as confusion and disappointment. This is of course only a way of saying that I agree with several of the observations made by Christopher Tolkien – prompted in part by perspicacious comments from Tom Shippey – in his discussion of the presentation of the history of the Elder Days in the Foreword to *The Book of Lost Tales*, Part I. "We do not actually see the Silmarils as we see the Ring," he wrote of *The Silmarillion* and its lack of "narrative urgency". And further: "The published work has no 'framework', no suggestion of what it is and how (within the imagined

---

[24] Cf. Noad 2000: 62, where a similar argument is made.

world) it came to be. This I now [1983] think to have been an error" (Tolkien 1983: pp. 4 and 5).

With the breakdown of the 'lost text technique', we are left with the other of the two main functions *The Silmarillion* was intended to have (cf. p. 142 above), namely as a mount for the 'great tales'. And as such, it works. We see what he was getting at – only largely, of course, not exactly, because he was constantly changing his mind and never finished anyway. We see why Tolkien felt and wanted some of his tales to be 'great'. We see how the tales interconnect, even when they are only "placed in the scheme, and sketched" (Tolkien 1981: 145). And because this was how the 'Silmarillion' started, as background to and outline of tales (supposedly) told more fully elsewhere, we get the tales in the characteristic form and style that some – far from all – readers find peculiarly appealing: laconic, dignified, calm, relating events from an exceedingly remote past with intriguingly or irritatingly little regard for modern novelistic convention.

For many readers, the successful, almost addictively effective, use of the 'lost text technique' is an important part of the special attraction of Tolkien's legendarium texts, *The Lord of the Rings* in particular. We are so used to seeing it applied consistently and skilfully that it can be hard to break the habit. But to fully enjoy *The Silmarillion* as a literature, I believe we should take a lost text holiday. Read *The Silmarillion* without trying to place it with Ælfwine or Bilbo or Pengolod or Rúmil or Númenórean or Gondorian loremasters. Take the position that the viewpoint is that of J.R.R. Tolkien wishing to present an audience of modern readers with a brief version of his 'legends' and stories of the Elder Days. You will probably regret that he never managed to finish it, but you will encounter stretches of his finest prose and some of his most powerful and poignant stories, dampened and sometimes obscured, to be sure, by only slightly veiled incompleteness and unavoidable inconsistencies, but not overwhelmed by them.

Nils Ivar Agøy, b. 1959, *dr. philos., cand. theol. & philol.*, professor of modern history at Telemark University College, Norway. He has written extensively on Tolkienian subjects. His publications in this field include *Mytenes mann: J.R.R. Tolkien og hans forfatterskap* (Oslo 2003) and, as editor, *Between Faith and Fiction: Tolkien and the Powers of His World* (Stockholm 1998). He has also translated *The Silmarillion, The Hobbit, Unfinished Tales* and *The Children of Húrin* into Norwegian. Tolkienian research interests include Tolkien and Christianity, Tolkien and cultural identity, and Tolkien's sub-creation theory.

References

Agøy, Nils Ivar, 1987, 'A Nodal Structure in J.R.R. Tolkien's Tales of the First Age?', in *Mythlore* No. 50, Vol. 13, pp. 22-25.

Flieger, Verlyn, 1997a, *A Question of Time: J.R.R. Tolkien's Road to Faërie*, Kent, Ohio: Kent State University Press.

—, 1997b, 'Whose Myth Is It?, in Nils Ivar Agøy (ed.): *Between Faith and Fiction: Tolkien and the Powers of His World*, Stockholm: Arda-sällskapet.

—, 2005, *Interrupted Music: The Making of Tolkien's Mythology*, Kent, Ohio: Kent State University Press.

—, 2006, 'Tolkien and the Idea of the Book', in Wayne G. Hammond and Christina Scull (eds.), *The Lord of the Rings 1954-2004: Scholarship in Honor of Richard E. Blackwelder*, Milwaukee, Wisconsin: Marquette University Press, pp. 283-299.

Noad, Charles, 2000, 'On the Construction of "The Silmarillion"', in Verlyn Flieger and Carl F. Hostetter (eds.), 2000, *Tolkien's Legendarium. Essays on The History of Middle-earth*, Westport, Connecticut: Greenwood Press, pp. 31-68.

Plotz, Richard: 'J.R.R. Tolkien talks about the discovery of Middle-earth, the origins of Elvish', in *Seventeen*, January 1967, pp. 92-93, 118.

Tolkien, Christopher, 1977, *The Silmarillion by J.R.R. Tolkien: A brief account of the book and its making*, Boston: Houghton Mifflin.

Tolkien, J.R.R, 1962, *The Adventures of Tom Bombadil*, London: Allen & Unwin.

—, 1977, *The Silmarillion*, London: Allen & Unwin.

—, 1981, *The Letters of J.R.R. Tolkien*, ed. by Humphrey Carpenter, London: Allen & Unwin.

—, 1983, *The Book of Lost Tales, Part I*, ed. by Christopher Tolkien, London: Allen & Unwin.

—, 1986, The Shaping of Middle-earth, ed. by Christopher Tolkien, London: Allen & Unwin.

——, 1987, *The Lost Road and Other Writings*, ed. by Christopher Tolkien, London: Allen & Unwin.

——, 1993, *Morgoth's Ring*, ed. by Christopher Tolkien. London: HarperCollins.

——, 1996, *The Peoples of Middle-earth*, ed. by Christopher Tolkien, London: HarperCollins.

——, 2004, *The Lord of the Rings*, 50th anniversary edition. Boston: Houghton Mifflin.

Turner, Allan, 2005, *Translating Tolkien: Philological Elements in The Lord of the Rings*, Frankfurt am Main: Peter Lang.

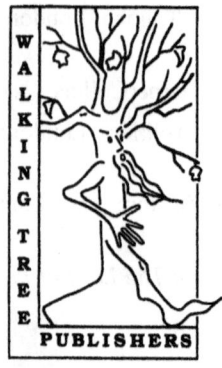

Walking Tree Publishers was founded in 1997 as a forum for publication of material (books, videos, CDs, etc.) related to Tolkien and Middle-earth studies. Manuscripts and project proposals can be submitted to the board of editors (please include an SAE):

Walking Tree Publishers
CH-3052 Zollikofen
Switzerland
e-mail: info@walking-tree.org
http://www.walking-tree.org

Cormarë Series

The *Cormarë Series* has been the first series of studies dedicated exclusively to the exploration of Tolkien's work. Its focus is on papers and studies from a wide range of scholarly approaches. The series comprises monographs, thematic collections of essays, conference volumes, and reprints of important yet no longer (easily) accessible papers by leading scholars in the field. Manuscripts and project-proposals are evaluated by members of an independent board of advisors who support the series editors in their endeavour to provide the readers with qualitatively superior yet accessible studies on Tolkien and his work.

News from the Shire and Beyond. Studies on Tolkien.
    Edited by Peter Buchs & Thomas Honegger. Zurich and Berne 2004. Reprint. First edition 1997. (Cormarë Series 1)

Root and Branch. Approaches Towards Understanding Tolkien.
    Edited by Thomas Honegger. Zurich and Berne 2005. Reprint. First edition 1999. (Cormarë Series 2)

Richard Sturch. *Four Christian Fantasists. A Study of the Fantastic Writings of George MacDonald, Charles Williams, C. S. Lewis and J.R.R. Tolkien.* Zurich and Berne 2007. Reprint. First edition 2001. (Cormarë Series 3)

Tolkien in Translation.
    Edited by Thomas Honegger. Zurich and Berne 2003. (Cormarë Series 4)

Mark T. Hooker. *Tolkien Through Russian Eyes.* Zurich and Berne 2003. (Cormarë Series 5)

Translating Tolkien: Text and Film.
    Edited by Thomas Honegger. Zurich and Berne 2004. (Cormarë Series 6)

Christopher Garbowski. *Recovery and Transcendence for the Contemporary Mythmaker: The Spiritual Dimension in the Works of J.R.R. Tolkien.* Zurich and Berne 2004. Reprint. First edition by Marie Curie Sklodowska University Press, Lublin 2000. (Cormarë Series 7)

Reconsidering Tolkien.
   Edited by Thomas Honegger. Zurich and Berne 2005. (Cormarë Series 8)

Tolkien and Modernity 1.
   Edited by Frank Weinreich & Thomas Honegger. Zurich and Berne 2006. (Cormarë Series 9)

Tolkien and Modernity 2.
   Edited by Thomas Honegger & Frank Weinreich. Zurich and Berne 2006. (Cormarë Series 10)

Tom Shippey. *Roots and Branches: Selected Papers on Tolkien by Tom Shippey.* Zurich and Berne 2007. (Cormarë Series 11)

Ross Smith. *Inside Language: Linguistic and Aesthetic Theory in Tolkien.* Zurich and Berne 2007. (Cormarë Series 12)

How We Became Middle-earth.
   Edited by Adam Lam & Nataliya Oryshchuk. Zurich and Berne 2007. (Cormarë Series 13)

Myth and Magic: Art According to the Inklings.
   Edited by Eduardo Segura & Thomas Honegger. Zurich and Berne 2007. (Cormarë Series 14)

The Silmarillion – Thirty Years On.
   Edited by Allan Turner. Zurich and Berne 2007. (Cormarë Series 15)

Martin Simonson. *The Lord of the Rings and the Western Narrative Tradition.* Zurich and Berne 2007, forthcoming.

Beyond Middle-earth: Tolkien's Shorter Works 1. Proceedings of the 4th Seminar of the Deutsche Tolkien Gesellschaft & Walking Tree Publishers Decennial Conference.
   Edited by Frank Weinreich & Margaret Hiley. Zurich and Berne 2007, forthcoming.

Beyond Middle-earth: Tolkien's Shorter Works 2. Proceedings of the 4th Seminar of the Deutsche Tolkien Gesellschaft & Walking Tree Publishers Decennial Conference.
   Edited by Margaret Hiley & Frank Weinreich. Zurich and Berne 2007, forthcoming.

Constructions of Authorship in and around the Works of J.R.R. Tolkien.
   Edited by Judith Klinger. Zurich and Berne, forthcoming.

Rainer Nagel. *Hobbit Place-names. A Linguistic Excursion through the Shire.* Zurich and Berne, forthcoming.

Tales of Yore Series

The *Tales of Yore Series* grew out of the desire to share Kay Woollard's whimsical stories and drawings with a wider audience. The series aims at providing a platform for qualitatively superior fiction with a clear link to Tolkien's world.

Kay Woollard. *The Terror of Tatty Walk. A Frightener.* CD and Booklet. Zurich and Berne 2000 (Tales of Yore 1)

Kay Woollard, *Wilmot's Very Strange Stone or What came of building "snobbits".* CD and booklet. Zurich and Berne 2001 (Tales of Yore 2)

Ossie felt the back of his neck go prickly....

www.ingramcontent.com/pod-product-compliance
Lightning Source LLC
Chambersburg PA
CBHW050818160426
43192CB00010B/1806